Can I Survive Widowhood

The struggle With Grief, Shock, and Reestablishing a New Life

by

Robbie Munn Bayler

Table of Contents

Introduction

One morning, I found myself staring at a cup of coffee, its steam disappearing into the cold air of an empty kitchen. It was the first morning I woke up alone after my husband passed away. Suddenly, it felt as if the world had stopped spinning. I couldn't remember how to breathe, much less how to live. The silence was broken only by the sound of my husband's dog sighing. My thoughts swirled with questions I didn't have answers to. How would I move forward? Could I survive this solitude? It was a moment of profound shock, one that many widows know too well.

This book was born from that moment and countless others like it. It is a guide, a companion for those who are navigating the turbulent waters of widowhood. I want to provide you with guidance, support, and hope, and perhaps help you avoid the many mistakes I made along this torturous path. The pages ahead are filled with real experiences and practical advice drawn from my own life and the lives of women I have met along the way.

Allow me to introduce myself. I have journeyed through life as a wife, a mother, a grandmother, and beyond. I have sung on stages, acted in plays, worked as an artist, and, as well, as a bookkeeper. I have traveled the world as a missionary. You may remember the movie "The Singing Nun"; well, I was often referred to as the singing missionary. I have also published my first book, a biblical novel. Each of these roles has shaped me, but it is my journey through widowhood that has brought me to you. As an author, I want to share my story and the stories of others to offer insights that might light your path.

Widowhood is fraught with challenges that are both common and deeply personal. Grief seems insurmountable, and loneliness can feel like an uninvited guest that refuses to leave. An identity crisis may loom large as you wonder who you are without your partner by your side. Financial insecurity might add to the weight you already carry. These struggles are real and valid. I acknowledge them here because I want you to know that you are not alone in facing them.

The structure of this book reflects the complexity of our journey. We will explore emotional resilience and how to cultivate strength amid despair, and as the Bible says, "Turn your mourning into dancing." We will discuss financial independence, offering advice to help you find stability. Furthermore, we will delve into the process of rebuilding your identity, uncovering who you are now and who you wish to become. Each chapter is designed to guide you through these themes, preparing you for the road ahead.

Throughout this book, you will find not only practical solutions but also inspirational stories. These narratives illustrate the possibilities of a fulfilling life after loss. They are stories of transformation and hope, meant to uplift and encourage you as you navigate your own path.

I invite you to see this book as more than a guide. It is a source of solidarity and shared experience. You are part of a larger community of resilient women who have faced similar trials and emerged stronger. Together, we can find strength in our shared stories and build a network of support.

As you turn these pages, I encourage you to embrace the journey that lies ahead. Widowhood is not an end but a beginning. It is an opportunity for personal growth and new possibilities. I want this book to serve as a beacon, guiding you toward a future filled with purpose and joy. Let us walk this path together with courage and openness to what comes next.

Dedication

Dedicated to the memory of my late Husband
John Kenneth Bayler the 3rd

Chapter 1

Confronting the Emotional Avalanche

Let's start by getting the worst part out of the way. I did not realize the full extent of my husband's illness until he died sitting in the chair beside me. I have been told that he didn't want me to worry. Really? Worry? No, I went into a shock so deep that for months on end, I didn't even want to live. A song would come on the radio, perhaps one that we both loved, and suddenly, the world would blur. My heart would ache with grief so deep it would feel like I was drowning. Tears were always ready to spill, and in those overwhelming moments, I understood how emotions could rise like a tidal wave, unexpected and uncontrollable. The only thing that kept me alive was knowing that my life doesn't belong to me, but to God. It isn't my choice; it is up to God and Him alone. In the ordinary, the extraordinary emerges with the force of grief. This chapter is about those emotional avalanches and how to navigate them.

Navigating the Emotional Roller Coaster

Emotions can be unpredictable. One moment, you might feel a glimmer of hope, and the next, a wave of sadness could crash over you. My first thought is always, how can I go on without him? Such fluctuations can be disconcerting, leaving you feeling unsteady. Acknowledging these shifts is important, as they are a natural part of the grieving process. You may experience emotional highs when remembering joyful moments, followed by lows as the reality of loss sinks in. Sudden waves of grief can be triggered by the smallest reminders: his favorite Psalm, a song, whether it was a favorite hymn or CCR, or a picture from one of our many travels. You realize that this era of your life has ended now. These emotions aren't linear or tidy, and accepting this unpredictability can be the first step toward understanding them.

To manage these swings, consider incorporating coping mechanisms into your daily life. Daily Bible study and prayer are excellent sources of peace and strength. Mindfulness and grounding exercises can help you stay present and calm. Simple breathing exercises can be particularly effective. Try inhaling deeply through your nose, holding for a moment, and then exhaling slowly through your mouth as you look up. This practice can anchor you, providing a moment of peace in the storm while keeping the tears at bay. Journaling is another powerful tool. By writing down your emotional states, you can begin to see patterns and gain insight into your grief. Mindfulness meditation, where you focus on the present moment without judgment, can also cultivate a sense of calm and stability. These practices create a buffer, allowing you to ride the emotional waves with a bit more ease.

Self-compassion is crucial during these times. Treat yourself with the same kindness and patience you would offer a dear friend. Self-compassion mantras can serve as gentle reminders to be tender with yourself. Phrases like "I am doing my best" or "It is okay to feel this way" can soothe your heart. Establishing self-care routines is equally essential. Whether it's a walk in nature, a warm bath, or a few moments of quiet reflection, these routines can provide comfort and help restore your sense of balance. Self-compassion is not just an act but an attitude that embraces your humanity in all its complexity.

Above all, don't fall into the trap of thinking you are more robust, better, or above this. Please remember that no one is, and I do mean no one. Even Christ cried during times of profound grief. It has been my observation that the people who deny or "shake off" grief are setting themselves up for a much longer and torturous time later.

Remembering the Scripture, Psalm 23, vs. 4, which states, "Yea though I walk through the valley of the shadow of death, You are with me. Your rod and Your staff, they comfort me," was a great source of comfort for me. He will be with us and comfort us if we let Him.

Connecting with others can also ease the weight of grief. Reach out to trusted friends and family members, those who offer a listening ear and a supportive shoulder. Sharing your feelings with someone who understands can lessen the burden. Like those mentioned by the National Institute on Aging, joining support groups can provide a sense of community and shared experience. These groups are spaces where you can express your emotions freely and find solace in the company of others navigating similar paths. Engaging with a community reminds you that you are not alone. Many understand and share your experiences.

Grief can feel like an isolating journey, but it doesn't have to be. By acknowledging the unpredictability of your emotions, employing coping strategies, practicing self-compassion, and seeking connection, you can navigate this emotional roller coaster with resilience and grace. These practices are not just about surviving widowhood but about finding a way to thrive amidst the chaos. This chapter, and indeed this book, is here to support you as you move through these tumultuous times, offering guidance and companionship along the way.

Understanding Grief's Many Faces

Grief is a complex emotion, and its manifestation can vary widely from one person to another. In the late 1960s, Elisabeth Kübler-Ross introduced the concept of the five stages of grief, a framework that many find helpful in navigating their own experiences. These stages— denial, anger, bargaining, depression, and acceptance—serve as a guideline, not a prescription. It's important to recognize that these stages are not straightforward, nor are they universally experienced. In the midst of denial, one might feel numb or disconnected, as if the loss hasn't really occurred. Perhaps, like me, you have had to be wheeled out of the hospital, crying out, "No, I don't want to live another day without him in my life." Anger might surface as a response to the perceived unfairness of the loss, while bargaining often involves negotiating with oneself or a higher power, hoping to reverse the situation. Depression can bring about profound sadness, a sense of emptiness that feels endless, and leave you feeling gutted. Finally, acceptance doesn't mean happiness but rather an acknowledgment of reality and a willingness to move forward, cherishing memories without being shackled by them. Try to find joy in remembering the happy times you shared with your loved one.

Each person's encounter with grief is unique, colored by personal history, relationships, and inner resilience. The path through grief is deeply personal, without a predetermined course. For instance, consider a woman I met at a support group who had lost her husband unexpectedly. She found herself in a prolonged state of denial, unable to move his belongings or change her daily routine. For her, anger came later, directed at the unpredictability of life itself. In contrast, another widow shared how anger was her initial response, a protective shield against the overwhelming sadness that followed. These stories remind us that there is no right or wrong way to grieve; each path is as individual as the person walking it.

Cultural perspectives can also shape how grief is expressed and processed. In some cultures, mourning is a communal affair, with rituals and ceremonies that provide structure and support. In others, grief may be a more private journey, with an emphasis on personal reflection and inner strength. These cultural practices can influence personal grief experiences, offering both solace and a framework for understanding. For example, in some African cultures, the bereaved are expected to express their sorrow publicly through wailing and ritualistic mourning, which can help release emotions and foster communal healing. In contrast, some Asian traditions may emphasize internalizing grief, focusing on meditation and quiet reflection as a path to peace. Understanding these diverse approaches can offer insight and compassion, helping us respect and honor the myriad ways in which grief is experienced.

To further explore the many faces of grief, I recommend seeking out resources that resonate with your personal experience. Books such as "On Grief and Grieving" by Kübler-Ross herself provide foundational insights into the grieving process. Articles and online resources, like those found on the National Institute on Aging's website, offer practical advice and support, acknowledging that grief is not a one-size-fits-all experience. The Sisterhood of Widows provides an online community where you can share stories and find comfort in shared experiences. These resources can provide additional perspectives and support, helping you navigate the complex landscape of grief with greater understanding and empathy.

Battling Overwhelming Loneliness

The silence of an empty home can be one of the most profound reminders of loss, a constant echo of what once was. The absence of a loved one leaves a tangible void that can be felt in every room, every corner. This sense of emptiness often manifests in what some call the "empty chair syndrome." You may find yourself glancing at the chair your partner used to occupy, expecting them to be there, only to be met with a painful reminder of their absence. In my case, I took one look at the chair my husband died in and said, "Please, get that chair out of here right now." Actually, as I look back on it, I think it was more of a scream. The once-comforting silence now feels oppressive, magnifying the loneliness that widowhood brings. This quiet home environment, once a sanctuary, can become a source of deep solitude, making it difficult to feel connected to the world outside. These feelings are valid and shared by many who stumble along this path.

Addressing loneliness requires intentional action, a conscious effort to reach out beyond the confines of your solitude. Don't feel condemned if it takes a while to reach this point. Each person travels this dark road at a different pace. One effective strategy is to engage in community activities. This can provide a sense of belonging and offer opportunities to connect with others who share similar interests. Volunteering is a wonderful way to combat loneliness; by helping others, you can find purpose and build meaningful connections. Whether it's reading to children at a local library or serving meals at a community center, such activities can fill the void with a sense of achievement and camaraderie. Participating in local clubs or groups, perhaps quilting, bridge, or Mahjong, centered around hobbies you enjoy, can also introduce you to new friends and experiences. These social interactions can be lifelines, pulling you out of isolation and into a network of support.

Building a support network is crucial for emotional well-being. It begins with reconnecting with old friends, those who knew you before and have shared history with you. Reach out, even if it's just a simple text or phone call. These relationships can provide comfort and a sense of continuity. In addition to rekindling past connections, consider engaging with online communities. The digital age offers a plethora of forums and groups where people come together to share experiences, advice, and encouragement. These virtual communities can be particularly helpful for those who find it challenging to meet people in person. They offer a safe space to express yourself and find understanding from others who are navigating similar life changes.

Should you decide to choose an online option, be careful, and I do mean meticulous, about divulging personal information. This can lead to a myriad of problems. There are dishonest people who prowl the internet for the sole purpose of looking for vulnerable people to take advantage of. Please keep in mind that we are truly vulnerable during this time of loss and despair.

While human connection is invaluable, it's equally important to cultivate a relationship with yourself. Embracing self-company can transform loneliness into solitude, a time for introspection and self-discovery. Solo hobbies, such as gardening, painting, or writing, can provide both distraction and enjoyment. These activities allow you to explore your interests and passions at your own pace, fostering a sense of independence and self-reliance. Engaging in creative pursuits, such as painting or cooking classes, can also be therapeutic, helping to process emotions and bring a sense of fulfillment. As you become comfortable with your own company, you'll find that solitude can be a source of strength and growth, rather than something to be feared.

Loneliness is a formidable adversary, but it is not insurmountable. With deliberate steps and an open heart, you can transform this challenging aspect of widowhood into an opportunity for connection and growth, both with others and with yourself. The journey to overcoming loneliness is not a solitary one; it's a path paved with shared experiences and mutual support. As you navigate this terrain, remember that you are not alone. There is a community waiting with open arms, ready to welcome you into a new chapter of life.

Coping with Unexpected Triggers

Grief is often like a shadow that lurks quietly, ready to surface at the most unexpected moments. Triggers are those subtle reminders that catch you unaware, pulling you back into the depths of your sorrow. They can be as ordinary as a date on the calendar or as surprising as a familiar tune that plays when you least expect it. Anniversaries and special dates hold particular power; they mark the passage of time and the absence of a loved one. These days can seem to magnify the loss, transforming what should be a celebration into a reminder of what is no longer. Similarly, places once shared, like a favorite restaurant or a park bench, can evoke memories that stir emotions long thought settled. A shared song drifting through the air can transport you back to happier times, leaving you grappling with a mix of nostalgia and pain. Recognizing these triggers is the first step in managing their impact. Try to remember the joy of that time rather than the pain of today. Remember that God promised to "turn our mourning into joy," and allow Him to do it. No, it isn't easy, but I promise you from personal experience that it is possible.

Preparation can offer a measure of control over these emotional ambushes. For known triggers, such as upcoming anniversaries, consider planning a meaningful way to honor the day. This could involve gathering with friends or family to share stories and memories, or perhaps spending the day engaged in an activity that your loved one cherished. Creating a calming environment in anticipation of these triggers can also be comforting. Light a candle, play soft music, or surround yourself with calming scents like lavender or chamomile. These small acts can create a sanctuary that offers peace amid turmoil. It's about acknowledging the trigger, not avoiding it, and finding ways to face it with a sense of readiness and calm.

Unexpected grief spikes can feel like a sudden storm. I remember going into our favorite restaurant for the first time and walking right into the arms of our favorite server. We just held each other and cried. So, people stared; let them. It was a time of healing and acknowledgment for both of us. No plan could have prepared either of us for that time, but having a plan, when possible, can ease the intensity of these moments. An emergency contact list is a simple yet effective tool. Write down the names of those you can turn to in times of need, whether for a listening ear or a comforting presence. Keep this list accessible, so you're never at a loss for support. Additionally, consider assembling a personal calming kit. Fill it with items that bring you comfort: a favorite book, a soothing tea blend, or a cherished photograph. These tangible reminders of comfort can provide immediate solace when emotions threaten to overwhelm you. The kit serves as a lifeline, grounding you when everything feels unsteady.

In these moments of vulnerability, it's crucial to remember your inherent strength. Reflect on past challenges you've overcome and recognize the resilience that lies within you. Each trigger faced and managed is a testament to your capability to endure and grow. As you navigate these emotional landscapes, remind yourself of the countless times you have risen above adversity. Stories of resilience abound in the lives of those around us. Consider the woman who found solace in her garden, tending to each plant with the same care she once gave to her partner, or the man who turned to painting, capturing memories on canvas as a way to honor his lost love. These stories, though personal, illustrate a universal truth: that within each of us lies the capacity to weather the storm and emerge stronger. These narratives serve as a beacon, gently guiding you toward the realization that you, too, possess this strength.

Triggers are an inevitable part of grieving, but they do not define your experience. By understanding their nature, preparing for their impact, and trusting in your resilience, you can navigate these emotional currents with confidence. The path may not always be smooth, but with each step, you affirm your ability to cope and continue moving forward.

Allowing Yourself to Feel Without Guilt

In the midst of grief, it is not uncommon to experience a spectrum of emotions that might catch you off guard. Joy, surprisingly, can be one of them. Imagine a moment when, during a family gathering or a simple walk in the park, a memory or a joke brings a smile to your face. Even laughter can bubble up, seemingly out of nowhere. Yet, just as quickly, guilt can cast a shadow over these moments of happiness. This is the paradox of grief—where joy and sorrow coexist, each one amplifying the complexity of the other. It is crucial to recognize that feeling happiness amidst sadness is not a betrayal of your loss. Rather, it is a testament to your capacity to hold both joy and grief simultaneously, a sign of resilience and the human spirit's ability to heal.

Guilt often emerges from the expectations placed upon us, both by society and ourselves. There is an unspoken script suggesting how one should grieve, how long it should last, and what it should look like. These societal expectations can be burdensome, whispering that moving forward means leaving loved ones behind. Alongside this, internalized pressure often acts as an invisible critic, questioning whether you're mourning "enough" or if your progress is too rapid. It's a heavy weight to carry, this guilt, but understanding its origins can begin to lighten the load. Recognize that guilt does not honor the memory of your loved one; instead, it holds you back from embracing life fully.

To move through guilt, self-forgiveness becomes an important ally. Consider engaging in practices that foster forgiveness and acceptance. Forgiveness meditation and/or prayer can be a gentle way to start, offering a space to acknowledge feelings without judgment. In a quiet setting, close your eyes and breathe deeply. Reflect on the guilt you feel, and with each breath, imagine releasing it into the air, allowing compassion to take its place. Another powerful exercise is writing a forgiveness letter. Address it to yourself, expressing understanding and empathy for your emotions. Allow this letter to be a reminder that you are worthy of happiness and peace, regardless of the grief you carry.

As you work through these feelings, it is important to celebrate the small victories along the way. Acknowledge each step forward, no matter how modest it may seem. Initiate a daily gratitude practice by noting three things you can thank God for each day, even on those days when grief feels overwhelming. It helps to give it to Him in prayer and ask Him to help you carry the heavy load. This practice can shift focus from what is lost to the small joys that persist. Likewise, keeping a journal of achievements, no matter how small, can serve as a testament to your strength and progress. Write about moments when you laughed, a task you completed, or a new experience you embraced. These entries will become a collection of triumphs, evidence of your ability to move forward without guilt.

Allowing yourself to feel without guilt is not about dismissing your grief. It is about embracing the full range of emotions that life brings, understanding that joy does not diminish love or loss. Embrace laughter when it comes; let happiness find its way back into your life. How often have you heard it said that laughter is the best medicine? It certainly has been for me. You are not dishonoring the past by living in the present. Instead, you are honoring both by acknowledging that they coexist within you. In this acceptance, there is healing, and with healing comes the freedom to live fully once more.

Finding Peace in Emotional Chaos

In the midst of emotional turmoil, finding peace can feel like an elusive goal. Yet, it is within reach through practices that center the mind and soothe the spirit. Mindfulness offers a path to this peace, providing techniques that bring calm even in the stormiest of times. Meditation, for instance, allows you a space within yourself where tranquility resides. Consider setting aside a few minutes each day to sit in stillness, focusing on your breath. Let each inhale and exhale ground you in the present moment, gently guiding your mind away from the chaos. Prayer, as well as guided meditation exercises, can be particularly helpful, as they offer structure and support, leading you step by step into a state of relaxation. These practices create a refuge, a place where peace is not just a fleeting visitor but a welcome resident.

Rituals add structure to our days, helping to cultivate a sense of peace and stability. A morning reflection routine, for example, can set a positive tone for the day ahead. Begin your day with quiet contemplation, perhaps sitting with a cup of warm tea and a thought-provoking book like the Bible. Let this time be yours, free from external demands. Similarly, evening gratitude journaling offers a space to reflect on the day's blessings. As the day winds down, jot down moments of gratitude, no matter how small. This practice shifts focus from sorrow to gratitude, highlighting the threads of joy woven into the fabric of daily life. Rituals are anchors, grounding you in the present while gently guiding you forward.

The simple ritual of caring for my husband's Australian Shepherd was both grounding and sorrowful. The sorrow came from her grief; she, too, had lost her best friend. She died within a year, bringing more loss and grief for me, but also thankfulness that she was not suffering. She, too, died of cancer.

Nature, with its timeless beauty and serenity, offers profound healing. Spending time outdoors can be a balm for the weary soul. Whether it's a leisurely walk through a nearby park or tending to a garden, these moments in nature provide solace and renewal. The simple act of walking amidst trees or flowers can awaken a sense of connection to the earth and life itself. Gardening, too, with its rhythm of planting and nurturing, parallels the journey of healing. As you care for the plants, observe the cycle of growth and renewal, and find comfort in the knowledge that life continues, and you are an integral part of it.

Affirmations can reinforce your inner strength and peace. Simple phrases, repeated daily, can shift your mindset and empower you. Consider incorporating affirmations into your morning routine or during moments of doubt. Phrases like "I am strong," "I am at peace," or "I am open to healing" can bolster your spirit. Write them down and place them where you'll see them often—on your mirror, your refrigerator, or even your phone. Let these affirmations be a gentle reminder of your resilience and your capacity for peace.

As you weave these practices into your life, remember that peace is not a destination but a process. It emerges from the small, deliberate choices we make each day to nurture our well-being. Each prayer, meditation session, and walk in nature brings you closer to a state of calm. And within this calm, you will find the strength to navigate life's challenges with grace and resilience. As you embrace these practices, know that peace is something you carry within, waiting to be uncovered and cherished.

Chapter 2

Reclaiming Financial Independence

I remember sitting at the kitchen table, surrounded by a sea of papers: bank statements, bills, and documents I had never paid much attention to before. My husband had always handled the finances, and suddenly, that responsibility fell solely on my shoulders. The numbers seemed to dance on the page, taunting me with their complexity. I felt overwhelmed and unsure of where to start. It was at that moment of frustration and uncertainty that I realized the importance of reclaiming financial independence. Understanding your financial landscape is not just about numbers; it's about empowerment and taking control of your future. Please don't do what I did—fall into a habit of "retail therapy." Amazon became too close a friend.

Assessing Your Financial Landscape

The first step in reclaiming financial independence is conducting a comprehensive financial inventory. Begin by gathering all financial documents and creating a detailed list of your assets, liabilities, and income sources. List every bank account, noting the balances and types of accounts you hold. Include checking accounts, savings accounts, and any certificates of deposit. Catalog your debts and loans, whether they are mortgages, car loans, or credit card balances. This inventory is a snapshot of your financial standing and serves as the foundation for future planning.

Next, compile a list of your income streams. Include all sources of income, such as wages, Social Security, pensions, rental income, or dividends from investments. This list should reflect your current financial reality, providing a clear picture of your monthly cash flow. Understanding where your money comes from is critical to making informed decisions about budgeting and spending. As you compile this information, consider creating a spreadsheet or using a financial app to keep everything organized. This will help streamline the process and make it easier to review and update as your financial situation evolves.

Once you've completed your inventory, it's time to evaluate your current financial health. One effective method is to calculate your debt-to-income ratio. This ratio compares your monthly debt payments to your monthly income and provides insight into your financial stability. To calculate it, divide your total monthly debt payments by your gross monthly income, then multiply by 100 to express it as a percentage. A lower percentage indicates a healthier financial state, while a higher one may suggest the need for debt reduction strategies. This evaluation helps you understand your financial strengths and weaknesses, setting the stage for targeted improvements.

Dealing with finances alone can be emotionally challenging, especially if it's a new responsibility. Financial anxiety is common, but there are strategies to overcome it. Start by acknowledging your feelings and permitting yourself to feel them without judgment. You are not alone in this struggle, and many have walked this path before you. Practice stress-reduction techniques, such as prayer, deep breathing, or meditation, to calm your mind and focus on the task at hand. Breaking financial tasks into smaller, manageable steps can also alleviate anxiety, making the process feel less daunting. Remember, financial independence is a journey, and each step you take is a step toward empowerment.

Setting initial financial goals is a vital part of reclaiming independence. Begin by establishing clear, realistic objectives for both the short and long term. For example, setting an emergency fund target can provide a safety net for unexpected expenses. Aim to save enough to cover three to six months of living expenses. This fund is your financial cushion, offering peace of mind and security. Additionally, consider creating a debt reduction plan. Prioritize paying off high-interest debts first, as they can quickly accumulate and become burdensome. By setting these goals, you create a roadmap to guide your financial decisions and actions.

Reflection Exercise: Financial Goals Checklist

- List your financial assets and liabilities. Include all accounts, loans, and debts.

- **Calculate your debt-to-income ratio.** Use this to assess your financial health.

- Identify emotional challenges related to finances. Write down any anxieties or concerns.

- **Set two short-term financial goals.** Consider emergency fund targets or debt reduction plans.

- **Set two long-term financial goals.** Think about future savings or investment strategies.

As you work through these steps, remember that reclaiming financial independence is a process that takes time and effort. Each small action you take contributes to a larger picture of self-reliance and empowerment. With patience and perseverance, you can navigate the complexities of your financial landscape, building a foundation for a secure and fulfilling future.

Budgeting for the New Normal

Crafting a budget that reflects your new reality is a crucial step in reclaiming financial independence. Begin by distinguishing between essential and non-essential expenses. Essentials include necessities such as housing, utilities, groceries, and transportation. These are the pillars of your budget, the expenses that must be prioritized each month. Non-essentials, on the other hand, encompass discretionary spending—dining out, entertainment, and leisure activities. Identifying these categories helps clarify where adjustments can be made. Start by listing all your monthly expenses, categorizing them as essential or non-essential. This exercise provides a clear picture of your spending habits and highlights potential areas for savings.

To streamline the budgeting process, consider using budgeting apps. These tools can simplify tracking your income and expenses, providing real-time updates on your financial standing. Apps like Mint, YNAB (You Need a Budget), and PocketGuard are user-friendly options that can help you manage your budget efficiently. They offer features such as automatic categorization of expenses, alerts for bill payments, and visual graphs to track spending patterns. These apps can be particularly helpful in maintaining discipline and ensuring that you adhere to your budget. Choose an app that resonates with your needs and commit to using it regularly.

Monitoring and adjusting your spending habits is an ongoing process. It's not enough to set a budget; staying on track requires vigilance and adaptability. Begin by tracking your expenses meticulously. An expense tracking sheet can be a useful tool for this purpose. At the end of each day or week, record your expenditures, noting both the amount and category. This practice not only keeps you accountable but also illuminates spending trends. Are there areas where you consistently overspend? Recognizing these patterns allows you to make informed adjustments. If you find that dining out is consuming more of your budget than expected, consider cooking at home more frequently or setting a limit on restaurant visits. Flexibility is key; your budget should evolve as your financial situation changes.

Implementing saving strategies can bolster your financial stability. Automatic savings transfers are a simple yet effective method to prioritize savings. Set up a recurring transfer from your checking account to a savings account each month. Treat this as a non-negotiable expense, just like your rent or mortgage. Even small contributions can accumulate over time, building a financial buffer for future needs. In addition, consider leveraging couponing and discount apps to reduce everyday expenses. Apps like Honey and RetailMeNot offer digital coupons and cashback opportunities, helping you save on groceries, clothing, and other purchases. These tools can stretch your dollars further, allowing you to allocate more resources toward savings.

Budgeting challenges are inevitable, but they can be managed with foresight and preparation. Unexpected expenses, such as car repairs or medical bills, can derail even the most carefully planned budget. To mitigate their impact, establish a contingency fund within your budget. Allocate a small portion of your income each month to this fund, creating a financial cushion for emergencies. When unexpected expenses arise, you'll have a dedicated resource to draw from, minimizing disruption to your primary budget. Additionally, review your budget periodically to ensure it remains aligned with your financial goals. Life circumstances change, and your budget should reflect these shifts. Regular reviews provide an opportunity to reassess priorities and make necessary adjustments.

Budgeting is not a one-time task but an ongoing commitment to financial health. By creating a realistic budget, monitoring spending habits, implementing savings strategies, and addressing challenges head-on, you can navigate your new financial landscape with confidence. This process empowers you to take control of your finances, providing the stability and security needed to focus on other aspects of life.

Understanding Investments and Savings

Deciphering the world of investments can feel like learning a new language. Terms like stocks, bonds, mutual funds, and ETFs might seem daunting, but understanding them can be empowering. Stocks represent ownership in a company; buying stocks means you're purchasing a piece of that company. The value of stocks can fluctuate based on the company's performance and market conditions. Bonds, on the other hand, are essentially loans you give to a corporation or government, which they repay with interest over time. Bonds are generally considered safer than stocks, but they offer lower returns. Mutual funds pool money from many investors to buy a diversified portfolio of stocks and bonds, managed by professionals. Exchange-Traded Funds (ETFs) are similar to mutual funds but are traded on stock exchanges like individual stocks. They often have lower fees and can be a flexible investment option. Understanding these basic concepts is crucial as you explore different investment opportunities.

Exploring various investment types can help you build a diverse portfolio that aligns with your financial goals and risk tolerance. Real estate investing involves purchasing properties to generate rental income or sell at a profit. It can be a stable investment, but it requires significant capital and management. Dividend stocks are shares of companies that pay regular dividends, providing a steady income stream. They are appealing to those seeking both growth and income. Each investment type carries its own set of risks and rewards. Real estate can be affected by market fluctuations, while dividends can change based on company performance. Weighing these factors against your financial goals and risk tolerance is key to making informed decisions. A well-rounded understanding of these options can guide your investment strategy.

Diversified savings serve as the backbone of financial stability. Short-term savings, such as high-yield savings accounts, offer a safe place to store funds with easy access and slightly higher interest rates than regular savings accounts. These accounts are perfect for building an emergency fund or saving for short-term goals. Long-term investments, like retirement accounts (IRAs and 401(k)s), are essential for securing your financial future. IRAs provide tax benefits and flexibility, while 401(k)s often include employer contributions, making them a powerful tool for retirement planning. Balancing both short-term savings and long-term investments ensures financial readiness for life's uncertainties and future aspirations. It's about creating a financial ecosystem that supports both immediate needs and long-term dreams.

Crafting a personal investment strategy involves aligning your investments with your unique financial goals and risk tolerance. Start by assessing how comfortable you are with risk. Are you willing to take on higher risk for potentially greater returns, or do you prefer stability even if it means lower returns? Your risk tolerance will guide your investment choices. Consider your financial goals: are you saving for a home, planning for retirement, or looking to generate passive income? Each goal may require a different approach. For example, aggressive growth strategies might suit long-term goals, while conservative options might be better for short-term needs. Diversification is also crucial; it spreads risk across various investments, reducing the impact of any single loss. Regularly review and adjust your strategy to ensure it remains aligned with your evolving goals and risk tolerance.

2.4 Navigating Insurance and Benefits

Navigating the realm of insurance can often feel like deciphering a foreign language. Yet, understanding your existing policies is critical for ensuring financial security. Begin by pulling out your life insurance policy. Review the coverage details, ensuring they adequately reflect your current needs. Consider whether the coverage amount aligns with your financial responsibilities and future goals. This policy is a safety net for your loved ones, offering peace of mind during uncertain times. Similarly, take a close look at your health insurance. Evaluate the types of coverage it provides, including hospital visits, prescription medications, and preventive care. Understanding the nuances of your health insurance plan can help you avoid unexpected expenses and ensure you're making the most of the benefits available to you.

Beyond your current policies, there may be other benefits and entitlements available that can ease financial burdens. Social Security survivor benefits, for instance, can provide significant support. These benefits are designed to offer financial assistance to those who have lost a spouse, helping to bridge the gap left by a reduced household income. To explore eligibility, contact the Social Security Administration or visit their website. They offer resources and guidance to help you understand the application process and calculate potential benefits. If your spouse were a veteran, you might also be eligible for veterans' benefits. These can range from pensions and healthcare to educational support. The Department of Veterans Affairs can provide detailed information on what benefits you may qualify for and how to claim them. Exploring these entitlements can provide much-needed financial relief, allowing you to focus on other aspects of life.

As your circumstances evolve, it's important to consider additional insurance needs. Long-term care insurance is one such consideration. This type of insurance covers services that assist with daily living activities, such as bathing, dressing, and eating, whether in a nursing home, assisted living facility, or at home. As healthcare costs continue to rise, long-term care insurance can protect your savings and provide quality care options. Evaluate whether this coverage aligns with your long-term financial goals and personal health history. Consulting with an insurance advisor can offer personalized insights and help you make informed decisions about adding or adjusting coverage.

Understanding the claims process is equally important in maximizing your insurance and benefits. Filing claims can be a complex, often overwhelming task, but knowing the steps can simplify the process. Begin by gathering all necessary documentation, such as policy numbers, medical records, and receipts for expenses. Organize these in a dedicated folder for easy access. Contact your insurance provider to initiate the claim, following their specific guidelines. <u>Keep a record of all communications, noting dates and individuals you speak with. This documentation can be invaluable if disputes</u> arise. Be prepared to answer questions and provide additional information as needed. Patience and persistence are key, as the claims process can be lengthy and extremely tedious. If challenges arise, don't hesitate to seek assistance from a financial advisor or insurance professional. Their expertise can guide you through the process and ensure you receive the benefits you're entitled to.

Navigating insurance and benefits can feel daunting, but it is a crucial component of financial security. With careful review, exploration of entitlements, and an understanding of the claims process, you can ensure that you and your loved ones are protected.

Creating a Sustainable Financial Plan

Building a cohesive financial plan is akin to assembling the pieces of a puzzle. Each element, whether it's budgeting, savings, or investments, plays a vital role in creating a complete picture of financial health. The first step is to integrate these elements into a cohesive plan that reflects your personal goals and circumstances. Start by reviewing your monthly budget, savings strategy, and investment portfolio. Look for ways they can complement each other. For instance, if your budget allows for a surplus, direct those funds into a high-yield savings account or investment vehicle that aligns with your goals. This integration ensures that every dollar is working toward your financial objectives, providing a clear path to financial security.

Regular financial review sessions are crucial to maintaining an effective plan. Set aside time each month to evaluate your financial progress. During these sessions, examine your income, expenses, savings, and investment performance. Are you on track to meet your goals? If not, identify the areas that need adjustment. These reviews are an opportunity to celebrate successes and address any challenges that arise. Consider keeping a financial journal to track these insights over time. Documenting your progress can reveal patterns and provide valuable lessons for future planning. Consistency is key; by making financial reviews a regular habit, you create a proactive approach to managing your finances, ensuring they remain aligned with your evolving needs.

Flexibility is a hallmark of a resilient financial plan. Life is unpredictable, and your financial circumstances will inevitably change. Income fluctuations can occur due to job changes, medical expenses, or unexpected events. To adapt, be prepared to adjust your budget and savings strategies as necessary. For example, if your income increases, consider boosting your savings contributions or paying off debt more aggressively. Conversely, if your income decreases, identify non-essential expenses that can be reduced or eliminated. Planning for major life events, such as retirement, education, or a significant purchase, requires foresight and adaptability. Set specific financial milestones for these events and adjust your plan as you move closer to them. This flexibility ensures your financial plan remains relevant and effective, regardless of life's twists and turns.

Prioritizing financial security is the bedrock of a sustainable plan. It provides peace of mind and confidence in your financial future. Consider security-focused financial products, such as emergency funds, insurance policies, and stable investment options, as foundational elements of your plan. An emergency fund serves as a financial cushion, covering unexpected expenses without derailing your budget. Insurance policies protect against unforeseen risks, safeguarding your assets and well-being. Stable investments, like bonds or dividend stocks, offer a steady income stream and reduce exposure to market volatility. By incorporating these elements into your plan, you build a financial safety net that supports both short-term needs and long-term goals.

Achieving financial independence requires diligence, adaptability, and a commitment to ongoing learning. As you refine your financial plan, remember that it's a dynamic process, one that evolves with your life and goals. Each step you take toward integrating, reviewing, and adapting your financial elements strengthens your financial foundation. It's about creating a plan that not only meets your current needs but also anticipates future challenges and opportunities. With a robust financial plan in place, you can navigate the complexities of life with confidence and security, knowing that your financial future is in your hands.

Seeking Professional Financial Guidance

Navigating the complexities of financial independence can sometimes feel overwhelming, particularly when faced with intricate investment decisions or the nuances of estate planning. These are moments when seeking the expertise of a professional can be invaluable. Consider reaching out to a financial advisor when you encounter situations that require an in-depth understanding of market trends, tax implications, or legal considerations that go beyond your experience. An advisor can offer personalized advice tailored to your specific circumstances, helping you make informed decisions that align with your long-term goals. Estate planning, for example, involves not just drafting a will, but also understanding how to protect and transfer your assets effectively. This process can be intricate, with many legal and financial variables to consider, and a professional can guide you through each step with clarity and assurance.

Choosing the right financial advisor is a critical decision that requires careful consideration. Start by looking for someone with solid qualifications, such as a Certified Financial Planner (CFP) credential. This certification indicates a high level of expertise and ethical standards in financial planning. Additionally, consider whether the advisor operates on a fee-only basis or earns commissions. Fee-only advisors charge a flat rate or hourly fee, ensuring their advice is unbiased and solely in your best interest. Commission-based advisors, on the other hand, may have incentives to recommend certain products, which can introduce potential conflicts of interest. It's important to ask about their fee structure up front to avoid surprises later. Transparency in fees and services is a hallmark of a trustworthy advisor, so don't hesitate to ask questions about how they are compensated and what services they offer.

Be especially vigilant in choosing your advisor. My husband and I thought that we were in safe hands; however, upon his death, it cost me $70,00.00.

Preparation is key to making the most of your financial consultations. Before meeting with an advisor, compile a list of questions that address your primary concerns and goals. Consider asking about their experience with clients in similar situations, their investment philosophy, and how they plan to help you achieve your financial objectives. Be ready to discuss your current financial situation openly, including your assets, liabilities, and any challenges you're facing. Bringing relevant documents, such as previous tax returns, account statements, and insurance policies, can provide a comprehensive picture that allows the advisor to offer more tailored advice. Taking notes during the meeting can help you remember key points and follow up on any action items discussed. Preparing thoroughly ensures that you make the most of your time and leave with a clear understanding of the next steps.

Understanding the roles and limitations of financial advisors is essential to setting realistic expectations. Advisors can offer valuable insights and strategies for managing your finances, from investment planning to retirement strategies. However, they cannot predict market movements or guarantee returns. Their role is to provide guidance based on available information and to help you navigate financial decisions. It's important to remember that while advisors can recommend strategies and products, the final decision always lies with you. They act as guides, not decision-makers. It's your financial future, and staying informed and engaged in the process is crucial. Knowing what advisors can and cannot do helps you make the most of their expertise while maintaining control over your financial path.

In this chapter, we've explored the steps to reclaim financial independence, from understanding your financial landscape to creating a sustainable plan. Seeking professional guidance is part of this journey, offering support and expertise when you need it most. As you continue to build your financial confidence, remember that you are not alone. With the right tools and support, you can navigate the complexities of your financial world with assurance, paving the way for future stability and peace. Next, we'll delve into redefining your personal identity, a crucial step in embracing life after loss.

Chapter 3

Redefining Personal Identity

I found myself staring into the mirror one morning, searching for the person I once knew. The reflection that gazed back was familiar, yet strangely foreign. It was a face marked by time and experience, yet it felt incomplete without my partner standing beside me. This moment of introspection led me to question: Who am I without my partner? The loss of a loved one can blur the lines of self-identity, leaving us adrift in a sea of uncertainty. The roles we played, the dreams we shared, and the future we envisioned together now seem distant. This chapter invites you to explore your identity beyond the confines of partnership and rediscover the essence of who you are.

Reflecting on your identity before marriage can be a profound exercise. Think back to the person you were, the passions you pursued, and the dreams that fueled your spirit. Journaling can be a powerful tool in this exploration. Start by writing about your past self, capturing your interests, values, and aspirations. Then, contrast these with your present self, noting how your experiences and relationships have shaped you. This practice can reveal the core threads that remain constant, even as life changes. It can also illuminate areas where new growth is possible, offering a roadmap for redefining your identity. Through this reflection, you may find that the person you were is still very much a part of who you are now, waiting to be reconnected.

The absence of a partner often creates a void, a silence that echoes through your days. This emotional void can be both disorienting and profound, as you grapple with the loss of shared routines and companionship. Acknowledging this void is the first step in understanding its impact. It is natural to feel confusion, as if the foundation of your identity has shifted. Allow yourself the space to feel this loss, for it is a testament to the love and connection you shared. Recognizing the depth of this void can also invite you to carefully fill it with new experiences and self-discovery, rebuilding your identity on your own terms.

Self-reflection can be a guiding light in this journey of rediscovery. Consider engaging in exercises that prompt you to explore your core values and beliefs. A "Values and Beliefs" worksheet can be a helpful tool. List the values that resonate most with you, such as compassion, honesty, or creativity. Reflect on how these values have influenced your choices and relationships. This exercise clarifies what matters most to you and serves as a compass for future decisions. Pair this with guided meditation and prayer focused on personal strengths. In a quiet space, center your thoughts on qualities you admire in yourself. Visualize these strengths as a source of inner power, ready to support you in this new chapter of life.

Understanding oneself is not only a process of reflection but also a powerful path to healing and personal growth. As you delve into the intricacies of your identity, you may find that self-discovery serves as a healing tool. It allows you to integrate the past with the present, creating a cohesive narrative of who you are. This process fosters resilience, empowering you to embrace life with renewed confidence. Self-discovery is not about discarding the past but about weaving it into the fabric of your current self, creating a richer, more nuanced identity. Embrace this journey of self-exploration with curiosity and openness, knowing that each insight brings you closer to understanding the unique tapestry of your identity.

Reflection Exercise: "Values and Beliefs" Worksheet

- **List your core values.** Consider the principles that guide your decisions and interactions.

- **Reflect on past experiences.** Write about moments when these values influenced your choices.

- **Identify your strengths.** Acknowledge the qualities you admire in yourself.

- **Visualize your ideal self.** Envision how these values and strengths will shape your future identity.

Rediscovering Your Passions and Interests

The echoes of childhood often hold the keys to our deepest joys. Think back to those carefree days when time seemed endless, and you engaged in hobbies purely for the love of them. Perhaps you loved to paint vibrant scenes, your imagination running wild with every brushstroke. Or maybe you found joy in the tactile satisfaction of knitting or crocheting, the yarn slipping through your fingers as you created something tangible and warm. Reconnecting with these interests can be a soothing balm, reminding you of who you were before life's responsibilities took center stage. Dust off that old easel or dig out those knitting or crochet needles. Allow yourself to immerse yourself in the simple pleasure of creation. Remember Snoopy's advice: "Sing like no one is listening and dance like no one is watching." These activities can reignite passions that may have lain dormant, waiting patiently for your return.

But life is not just about looking back; it's also about the excitement of discoveries. Consider stepping beyond the familiar by exploring new activities that pique your curiosity. Perhaps there's a local pottery class that has always intrigued you, where you can mold clay into forms that reflect your inner world. Or maybe an online photography course could open a new lens through which you see the world. Such pursuits can lead to newfound passions, providing a fresh sense of purpose and excitement. Engaging in these activities enriches your life and expands your horizons, introducing you to new communities and perspectives. The thrill of learning something new can be invigorating, filling your days with anticipation and wonder.

Creative expression holds a unique power to foster self-understanding and emotional release. Writing poetry or stories allows you to explore your internal landscape, giving voice to thoughts and feelings that might otherwise remain silent. The act of putting pen to paper can be cathartic, transforming emotions into art. Similarly, painting or drawing can serve as a meditative practice, where the focus is not on the outcome but the process itself. Each stroke of the brush or pencil becomes a dialogue between you and the canvas, capturing the essence of your emotions. These creative outlets offer a safe space to express yourself, explore the depths of your psyche, and release the tension that often accompanies grief. They are means of healing, ways to understand yourself more deeply and communicate with the world around you.

Adopting a mindset of exploration can transform how you approach life. View each day as an opportunity to try something new, step outside your comfort zone, and embrace the unknown. Consider setting a personal challenge to "try something new" regularly, whether it's cooking a new recipe, visiting a museum, or taking a different route on your daily walk. This mindset encourages curiosity and openness, allowing you to see the world through fresh eyes. It invites you to be an active participant in your own life, constantly discovering and evolving. By embracing this exploratory attitude, you cultivate a sense of adventure and possibility, enriching your life rather than merely plodding through it.

Setting Personal Goals for Growth

Setting personal goals is like planting seeds in a garden. Each goal represents a seed, holding the potential for growth and transformation. To nurture these seeds, a structured approach is essential. The SMART goals framework can be a valuable tool in this process. SMART stands for Specific, Measurable, Achievable, Relevant, and Time-bound. By setting goals that align with these criteria, you ensure they are clear and attainable. For instance, instead of a vague goal like "be healthier," a SMART goal would be "walk 30 minutes every day for the next month." This goal is specific in its activity, measurable by time, achievable within your current routine, relevant to improving health, and time-bound with a one-month timeframe. By crafting goals in this manner, you create a roadmap for success, guiding your efforts with precision and purpose.

Personal growth is a lifelong journey, and setting goals is integral to this ongoing development. Goals act as signposts, guiding you toward your aspirations and helping you track your progress. They encourage you to step beyond your comfort zone, fostering resilience and adaptability. Long-term goals, like learning a new language or achieving a professional milestone, provide a vision for the future. They inspire you to dream big and pursue your passions with determination. Short-term goals, on the other hand, offer immediate, actionable steps that build momentum. These can be as simple as reading a book each month or trying a new recipe weekly. Together, these goals create a balanced approach to growth, weaving long-term aspirations with present-day actions.

Along the path to achieving your goals, obstacles are inevitable. They may take the form of procrastination, fear of failure, or unexpected challenges. Recognizing these potential hurdles allows you to prepare strategies for overcoming them. Procrastination, for instance, can be tackled by breaking tasks into smaller, manageable steps. If your goal is to declutter your home, start with one drawer or room at a time, setting a timer for 15-minute intervals. This focused approach reduces an overwhelming feeling and fosters a sense of accomplishment. Fear of failure can be mitigated by reframing setbacks as learning opportunities. Each challenge presents a chance to gain insight, refine your approach, and strengthen your resolve. Embrace these lessons as stepping stones on your path to success, knowing that each effort brings you closer to your goal.

Celebrating progress is as vital as setting goals themselves. Acknowledging your achievements, no matter how small, reinforces your commitment and boosts your motivation. Consider keeping a "success journal," where you record your accomplishments, reflecting on the journey and the growth you've experienced. This journal serves as a tangible reminder of your capabilities, inspiring confidence and perseverance. Rewarding yourself for reaching milestones can also be a powerful motivator. Whether it's treating yourself to a favorite activity, indulging in a special meal, or simply taking a moment to savor the satisfaction of progress, these rewards honor your dedication and hard work. They remind you that each step forward, no matter how incremental, is a victory worth celebrating.

Personal growth is not a destination but an ongoing process of self-discovery and evolution. Through thoughtful goal-setting, you cultivate a garden of possibilities, nurturing your potential and embracing the richness of life. As you navigate the path of growth, remember that each goal, each effort, and each celebration contributes to the vibrant tapestry of your life.

Embracing New Roles and Responsibilities

The landscape of life can shift dramatically after losing a partner, leaving you to navigate a world of new roles and responsibilities. Suddenly, tasks and decisions that were once shared now rest solely on your shoulders. Managing household duties becomes a daily challenge, from ensuring bills are paid on time to fixing the leaky faucet in the kitchen. These chores, once routine, may now feel overwhelming; yet mastering them brings a sense of accomplishment and control. Similarly, financial responsibilities demand attention. Perhaps you were not the primary budgeter, and now you find yourself deciphering bank statements and investment accounts. It's a learning curve, yet each step forward is a testament to your resilience.

Adapting to these new roles requires patience and strategy. Time management becomes your ally, helping to organize tasks so that life feels less chaotic. Consider creating a weekly planner or to-do list, breaking larger tasks into smaller, manageable steps. Prioritizing tasks not only alleviates stress but also provides clarity and focus. Delegating tasks is another powerful tool. It's okay to ask for help, whether from family or friends. They may assist with errands or lend a hand with more complex tasks. Seeking help is not a sign of weakness; it is a recognition that you are not alone. Community resources can also be invaluable. Local organizations often offer support groups or workshops to help you develop the skills you need. Libraries or community centers frequently hold classes on everything from cooking to basic home repair, providing a space to learn and grow.

Embracing these roles can lead to empowerment, fostering an increased sense of personal growth and independence. Each new skill you acquire adds to your toolbox, strengthening your confidence and self-reliance. You begin to see yourself not just as someone trying to manage, but as someone who is thriving. This empowerment is transformative. As you navigate these responsibilities, you may find that your perspective shifts from "I must" to "I can." This change in mindset can be liberating, allowing you to see possibilities rather than burdens.

Support is a crucial component in this transition. Building a network of friends, family, and community members who understand your situation can provide a lifeline of encouragement and advice.

These connections offer more than just practical assistance; they provide emotional support, reminding you that you are part of a larger community. Engaging with others who have faced similar challenges can be particularly comforting. Their experiences offer insights and reassurance, helping you to feel less isolated. Online forums and support groups can also be a source of connection, especially if you find it difficult to attend in-person gatherings. These spaces allow you to share your experiences, seek advice, and offer support to others, creating a sense of solidarity and understanding.

Perhaps, like me, you don't drive; consider delivery services for groceries or prescriptions by mail. There are also insurance companies that will provide rides to and from doctor visits. As the shock wears off and clearer thinking returns, you can research these possibilities of ways to make your life easier and more manageable.

In the midst of adjusting to new roles and responsibilities, remember that growth and change are part of life's ebb and flow. Each challenge faced and overcome becomes a building block of personal strength. You may discover capabilities you never knew you had, and with each success, your confidence will grow. This evolution is not about forgetting the past, but about honoring it by creating a vibrant, fulfilling present. Embracing these changes with an open heart and mind can lead to unexpected joys and accomplishments, weaving a new tapestry of life that is rich with experience and possibility.

Building Self-Confidence and Autonomy

Standing at the crossroads of life without a partner can sometimes shake the very foundation of self-belief. Confidence may feel like a distant memory, buried under layers of doubt and uncertainty. Yet, the journey back to self-assurance begins with a simple yet powerful step: belief in oneself. Confidence acts as an inner compass, guiding you through decisions and challenges with clarity and assurance. It's the quiet voice that says, "I can do this," even when the world feels overwhelming. Positive affirmations can nurture this belief, serving as daily reminders of your inherent strength and worth. Consider starting each day with affirmations that resonate with you, such as "I am capable," "I am worthy," or "I am enough." These words, repeated with intention, can slowly dismantle doubt, building a solid foundation of self-trust.

To bolster self-confidence, practical exercises can provide both structure and encouragement. I like to start my day singing an old chorus, "Give Thanks With a Grateful Heart." Daily mirror exercises are a simple yet effective way to reinforce self-esteem. Stand before a mirror, look into your eyes, and speak words of encouragement aloud. These practices, though they may feel awkward at first, can gradually shift your perception, allowing you to see yourself through a lens of kindness and appreciation. Another avenue for building confidence is through self-confidence workshops. These workshops, often available through church community centers or online platforms, offer a supportive environment to explore personal strengths and overcome limitations. Engaging with others on a similar path can provide both validation and inspiration, reinforcing that self-confidence is not just a destination but a continuous practice of self-love and acceptance.

Self-reliance is another pillar of personal growth, empowering you to navigate life's challenges independently. Developing decision-making skills is integral to this process. Start by making small decisions on your own, whether it's choosing a meal or planning a weekend activity. Gradually increase the complexity of these decisions, building confidence in your ability to assess situations and act accordingly. With each decision, you gain a more profound understanding of your values and priorities, strengthening your sense of autonomy. Over time, this practice becomes second nature, equipping you with the tools to face larger, more complex challenges with poise and assurance.

Autonomy plays a crucial role in shaping a strong personal identity. It's about carving out a space where your voice is the guiding force and your choices reflect your true self. Autonomy allows you to explore who you are outside external influences, fostering a deeper sense of self-awareness and authenticity. With autonomy comes the freedom to pursue passions, set boundaries, and make choices that align with your values. This self-discovery enriches your life, creating a tapestry of experiences woven from your own desires and aspirations. As you embrace autonomy, you may find a newfound sense of purpose and fulfillment, as well as a deeper appreciation for your unique journey.

Crafting Your Personal Narrative

Imagine your life as a tapestry, each thread a different story, each color a unique emotion. You possess the power to weave this tapestry, crafting a narrative that is yours and yours alone. It's not just about recounting events but about finding meaning in them. Viewing your life as a story allows you to shape it with intention. Start by writing a personal memoir—not for publication, but for yourself. Recount the chapters of your life, focusing on pivotal moments and the lessons they've imparted. This process isn't about crafting a perfect tale; it's about honoring your experiences and acknowledging their impact on who you are today. As you pen these memories, you might find that the act of writing brings clarity, helping to piece together the puzzle of your life.

In tandem with writing, a vision board can serve as a visual representation of your aspirations and dreams. Gather images, words, and symbols that resonate with you, arranging them in a way that reflects your desired path. This board acts as a compass, guiding you toward the life you envision. It serves as a daily reminder of your goals, helping to keep them at the forefront of your mind. The combination of writing and visualizing creates a powerful synergy, engaging both the mind and heart in crafting your personal narrative. Together, these tools allow you to see your life as a dynamic story, one that evolves with each new experience.

The power of narrative lies in its ability to heal and transform. When you craft your personal story, you engage in emotional processing, turning chaos into coherence. This act of storytelling helps to organize your thoughts and feelings, providing a sense of control amidst uncertainty. It allows you to make sense of past events, integrating them into a cohesive whole. This process can be profoundly therapeutic, offering a safe space to explore emotions and gain perspective. By shaping your narrative, you reclaim agency over your life, transforming experiences into opportunities for growth and understanding. The stories we tell ourselves shape our reality, influencing how we perceive and interact with the world.

Recognizing yourself as the protagonist of your story empowers you to take ownership of your life. You are not a passive observer but an active participant, capable of directing the course of events. Embrace this role with confidence, knowing that you alone can write new chapters filled with possibility and hope. In viewing yourself as the central character, you affirm your worth and agency, reminding yourself that your story is valuable and unique. This perspective fosters a sense of empowerment, encouraging you to embrace challenges as opportunities for learning and growth. It reinforces the notion that you are the author of your fate, capable of crafting a narrative that reflects your deepest desires and aspirations.

To aid in this creative process, consider utilizing tools and techniques designed to help construct your personal story. Storyboarding can be an effective method for organizing personal milestones, allowing you to map out significant events and their impact on your journey. This visual representation helps to identify patterns and connections, offering insights into your personal evolution. Reflective journaling prompts can further enhance this exploration, guiding you to delve deeper into your thoughts and emotions. Questions such as "What pivotal moments have shaped my identity?" or "How have I grown through adversity?" can spark introspection and insight. These tools serve as guides, helping you to craft a narrative that is both authentic and meaningful.

As this chapter concludes, you have explored the profound impact of crafting your personal narrative. This journey of storytelling does not end here—instead, it continues to unfold, offering endless opportunities for self-discovery and healing. As you shape your narrative, remember that you are not alone. Countless others are weaving their stories, creating a rich tapestry of shared experiences and wisdom. Together, we embrace the power of our stories, finding strength and solace in their telling. Let this chapter be a stepping stone, guiding you toward a life of purpose and fulfillment. As we move forward, we will delve into building supportive communities, exploring how connection can further enrich and empower our lives.

Chapter 4

Building a Supportive Community

The warmth of a shared smile can light up the darkest of days. I recall a time when a simple coffee date with a friend turned into an afternoon of laughter and stories, a brief respite from the loneliness that often enveloped me. It was at that moment that I truly understood the power of community, of having a network of people who can stand by you through life's ups and downs. Widowhood can feel like an isolating experience, yet it is within our reach to build a supportive community that offers comfort, empathy, and understanding. This chapter is dedicated to helping you find your tribe, those individuals who can walk alongside you, offering companionship and support as you navigate this new chapter of life.

A supportive network is indispensable for emotional well-being. It provides a safety net, a group of individuals who understand and empathize with your experiences. Emotional support is a cornerstone of healing, offering a space where you can express your feelings without judgment. This support often manifests in shared experiences and understanding. Being surrounded by individuals who have faced similar challenges can be incredibly validating. They know the weight of grief and the courage it takes to move forward. This shared understanding fosters a sense of belonging, a reminder that you are not alone in your journey.

To build such a network, start by identifying potential support figures in your life. Community groups and clubs are excellent starting points. They provide a structured space to meet like-minded individuals who share your interests. Whether it's a book club, a gardening group, or a fitness class, these gatherings offer opportunities to connect and form meaningful relationships. Interest-based meetups, often found through local listings or online platforms, can also be fruitful. These meetups focus on specific hobbies or activities, attracting individuals who share a common passion. By participating in these groups, you create a foundation for connections that can blossom into lasting friendships.

In a supportive community, the role of mutual support cannot be overstated. It's a reciprocal relationship where giving and receiving support go hand in hand. Offering your time, a listening ear, or a helping hand strengthens bonds and enriches your own experience. There is a unique sense of fulfillment that comes from being there for others, from knowing that your presence can make a difference. This reciprocity builds trust and deepens connections, creating a network that is both resilient and nurturing. It's a reminder that support is not a one-way street; it's a shared journey of empathy and care.

Proactive community engagement is key to cultivating these connections. It requires stepping out of your comfort zone and actively seeking out opportunities to engage with others. Local events, whether cultural festivals, workshops, or volunteer activities, present ideal opportunities to meet new people. Attending these events with an open heart and mind can lead to unexpected friendships and connections. It's about being present, about showing up and participating in the world around you. This engagement enriches your life and contributes to the community, creating a ripple effect of positivity and support.

Reflection Exercise: Identifying Your Support Network

- **List existing support figures.** Consider friends, family, and acquaintances who offer support.

- **Explore community groups.** Research local clubs or activities that align with your interests.

- **Identify opportunities for mutual support.** Reflect on ways you can support others in your network.

- **Plan community engagement.** Choose an upcoming event to attend and connect with others.

Navigating Social Events with Confidence

Stepping into a room full of people can be daunting, especially after experiencing loss. The hum of conversation, the clinking of glasses, and the swirl of laughter can feel overwhelming. Yet, social events hold the promise of connection and the potential to break the cycle of isolation. Preparing for these gatherings can boost your confidence and ease any anxiety you might feel. Start by equipping yourself with conversation starters. Think of a few topics that interest you or questions that invite others to share their stories. Simple prompts like "Have you read any good books lately?" or "What do you enjoy doing in your spare time?" can open the door to meaningful interactions. Bringing a friend for support can also bolster your confidence. A familiar face offers comfort and can help ease you into the social atmosphere, providing a sense of security as you navigate the room.

Attending social events offers more than just an opportunity to fill an evening; it opens doors to building new friendships and developing social skills. Engaging with others in these settings can lead to connections that enrich your life with diverse perspectives and experiences. Each conversation is a chance to learn something new, to discover common interests, and to forge bonds that might blossom into lasting friendships. Socializing also hones your ability to communicate and empathize, skills that are valuable in all areas of life. As you interact with different people, you become more adept at reading social cues, listening attentively, and expressing yourself with clarity and confidence. These skills can not only enhance your personal interactions but also boost your self-assurance, making you more comfortable in various social settings.

Social anxiety is a common challenge, particularly when reentering social circles after a period of solitude. The fear of judgment, the pressure to impress, and the apprehension of revealing your true self can all contribute to feelings of anxiety. To manage these emotions, consider incorporating calming techniques into your routine. Breathing exercises are simple yet effective tools for calming your nerves. Before entering a social setting, take a few moments to focus on your breath. Inhale deeply through your nose, hold for a moment, and then exhale slowly through your mouth. This rhythmic breathing can help quiet your mind and steady your heart, grounding you in the present moment. Setting personal boundaries is another important strategy. Decide in advance how long you wish to stay at an event and with whom you feel comfortable engaging. Knowing your limits can alleviate pressure and make socializing feel more manageable, as long as you stick to your plan.

Approaching social interactions with curiosity and openness can transform your experience. Embrace each encounter as an opportunity to learn and grow. This mindset welcomes new experiences, encouraging you to explore beyond your comfort zone. When you view social events through a lens of curiosity, you shift your focus from fear to discovery. Every person you meet has a unique story, a wealth of knowledge, and insights to share. By listening with an open mind, you expand your understanding of the world and your place within it. This perspective fosters a sense of adventure, turning socializing into a journey of exploration. As you navigate these events, allow yourself the freedom to be present, to engage fully, and to enjoy the richness of human connection.

Engaging with Online Support Groups

In today's digital age, the internet offers a vast array of communities where you can find connection and support without leaving the comfort of your home. Online support groups have become havens for people seeking understanding and empathy, especially during times of profound change. The beauty of these digital spaces lies in their ability to bring together diverse perspectives from around the world, offering a rich tapestry of experiences that can broaden your understanding and provide unique insights. Within these groups, anonymity and privacy allow you to share your thoughts and feelings without fear of judgment, offering a safe space to express emotions and explore new ideas. This combination of diversity and privacy creates a nurturing environment where personal growth and healing can flourish.

Finding the right online community is crucial to ensuring you receive the support and connection you need. Start by exploring widowhood support forums, which are specifically designed to address the unique challenges of losing a spouse. These forums often feature discussion threads, advice columns, and personal stories that can provide comfort and guidance. Social media groups, such as those on Facebook, also offer platforms for connection. These groups often have moderators who ensure that discussions remain respectful and focused, creating a positive and supportive atmosphere. When searching for an online community, consider what aspects are most important to you, whether it's the level of activity, the topics discussed, or the tone of the conversations. By aligning your needs and values with the group's dynamics, you can find a community that feels like a second home.

Interacting in online spaces requires a certain level of etiquette to ensure that the community remains a welcoming and supportive environment for everyone. Active listening is a fundamental aspect of this etiquette. When engaging with others, take the time to read their posts carefully, acknowledging their experiences and emotions. Respond with empathy, offering support and understanding rather than advice unless specifically requested. This practice fosters a sense of connection and trust, allowing members to feel heard and valued. Empathy is the cornerstone of these interactions, creating a space where individuals can share openly and authentically. By approaching each conversation with compassion and respect, you contribute to a positive and nurturing online community.

Online support groups offer a wealth of resources that can enhance your healing journey. Webinars are a popular feature, providing expert insights on topics like grief management, self-care, and personal development. These sessions offer practical advice and strategies that you can apply to your own life. Virtual meetups are another valuable resource, allowing members to connect in real-time through video calls. These meetups provide an opportunity to engage more deeply with other members, fostering a sense of camaraderie and shared experience. They also offer a chance to discuss specific challenges or goals, receiving feedback and encouragement from others who understand your journey. By participating in these resources, you can gain new perspectives and tools to support your growth and healing.

Resource List: Top Online Support Groups for Widowhood

- **Widowed Village by Soaring Spirits International**: Offers forums, virtual meetups, and workshops.

- **Grief in Common**: Provides resources, live chats, and individual coaching.

- **Grief Anonymous:** Features social media-based support through Facebook groups.

- **Grouport Therapy:** Offers online group therapy for grief and loss.

These groups offer various support options, allowing you to choose the format and focus that best suit your needs. Whether you prefer structured webinars or casual meetups, these communities provide a wealth of opportunities to connect, learn, and grow. They serve as a reminder that you are not alone, offering a network of individuals who understand and support your journey.

Reconnecting with Old Friends and Family

Reconnecting with old friends and family can feel like opening a long-forgotten book, each page filled with shared history and cherished memories. These relationships form the tapestry of our lives, woven with moments of laughter, support, and understanding. In times of change, reaching back to these connections can provide a sense of stability and warmth. Friends and family often hold pieces of our past, reflecting parts of ourselves that might feel lost in the present. They remind us of who we were and offer a bridge to who we can become. Rebuilding these ties can be a source of strength and comfort, offering familiar companionship as you navigate this new phase of life.

Reaching out to old contacts requires a delicate balance of intention and openness. Begin by sending thoughtful messages, whether through a handwritten note or a heartfelt email. Express genuine interest in their lives and share a bit about your own journey. A simple, "I've been thinking of you and would love to catch up," can open the door to rekindling a connection. These messages set the stage for deeper interactions, laying the groundwork for future communication. Once contact is reestablished, consider planning casual meetups. A coffee date or a walk in the park can provide a relaxed setting for conversation and reconnection. These low-pressure environments allow for natural dialogue, creating space for the relationship to flourish anew.

Challenges may arise as you reconnect with old friends and family, particularly if past conflicts remain unresolved. Time apart can sometimes amplify misunderstandings or hurt feelings. Addressing these issues head-on is crucial for rebuilding a healthy relationship. Approach conversations with empathy and a willingness to listen, acknowledging past grievances while focusing on the present. It's important to express your feelings honestly but also to be open to their perspective. This mutual understanding can pave the way for healing and forgiveness, allowing both parties to move forward with a clean slate. Remember, it's okay to set boundaries and take things at a pace that feels right for both of you.

Open communication is the lifeblood of any relationship, old or new. It's the key to rebuilding trust and fostering genuine connection. As you rekindle relationships, prioritize clear and honest dialogue. Share your needs and boundaries openly, and encourage your friends and family to do the same. This transparency creates a foundation of trust, ensuring that both parties feel respected and understood. By expressing your expectations and listening to theirs, you create a space where both parties can thrive. It's not just about speaking but also about truly hearing and valuing each other's words. This level of communication can transform old relationships, infusing them with new life and meaning.

Creating New Social Circles

Finding new friends can be like discovering a new piece of yourself. Each new connection brings fresh perspectives and a burst of energy that can invigorate your life. It's easy to get comfortable in familiar circles, but expanding your social horizons can introduce you to ideas and experiences you might never have considered. New friendships can spark joy and curiosity, encouraging you to explore parts of the world you haven't yet seen. They bring diversity of thought, and with it, the opportunity to grow in unexpected ways. These connections can breathe new life into your routine, transforming the everyday into something extraordinary.

Meeting new people might seem daunting, but it can also be a rewarding adventure. Start by joining hobby groups or classes that align with your interests. Whether it's a painting class, a hiking club, or a cooking workshop, these spaces naturally attract people with similar passions. Engaging in a shared activity provides common ground and eases the initial awkwardness of introductions. Volunteering for local causes is another excellent way to meet like-minded individuals. Not only does it allow you to contribute positively to your community, but it also connects you with others who value service and engagement. These environments foster authentic interactions, making it easier to forge meaningful connections. You're not just meeting people; you're joining a community with shared goals and values.

Diversity in social circles enriches your life in countless ways. Friends from different backgrounds bring unique cultural insights and experiences that can broaden your understanding of the world. Through these friendships, you might discover new cuisines, celebrate different traditions, or gain fresh perspectives on global issues. This cultural exchange enhances empathy and promotes a more inclusive worldview. By seeking out diverse friendships, you create a vibrant tapestry of connections that reflect the beauty of our global community. Engaging with people from varied walks of life challenges your assumptions and encourages personal growth, leading to a more well-rounded and informed perspective.

Forming new friendships involves a series of stages, each offering its own rewards and challenges. Initially, acquaintances are formed through casual conversations and shared interests. This stage is about testing the waters, seeing if there's a mutual connection worth pursuing. As you spend more time together, you begin to build trust and familiarity, moving from acquaintances to friends. This stage is marked by a more in-depth understanding of each other's lives and personalities. Finally, as the friendship strengthens, it may develop into a profound bond where you support each other through life's ups and downs. Understanding these stages helps manage expectations and encourages patience as relationships unfold. Friendships, like gardens, require time and care to flourish. Each interaction, each moment of shared laughter or support, contributes to the growth of a lasting connection.

Balancing Solitude and Socialization

Solitude is often misunderstood. In a world that celebrates social connections, it can be mistaken for loneliness. Yet, spending time alone can be incredibly enriching. It offers a unique space for reflection and self-discovery, allowing you to connect with your thoughts and emotions without distraction. During these quiet moments, you can explore your innermost desires, fears, and dreams. Solitude provides the clarity to understand who you are and what truly matters to you. It acts as a mirror, reflecting your true self to you, free from external influences or societal expectations. This self-awareness is the foundation of personal growth, enabling you to make decisions that align with your values and aspirations.

Balancing solitude with socialization requires intention and effort. One effective strategy is to schedule social activities with the same commitment you would apply to work or family obligations. By setting specific times for social engagements, you ensure that they are an integral part of your life, not an afterthought. This approach allows you to enjoy social interactions fully, knowing that you have also allocated time for yourself. Equally important is setting personal downtime, moments when you can recharge and reflect. Whether it's a morning walk in nature or an evening spent reading, these periods of solitude are vital for maintaining your mental and emotional health. They provide the balance needed to engage with others meaningfully, ensuring that your social interactions are fulfilling rather than draining.

Mindful socialization is about choosing quality over quantity in your social engagements. It involves being intentional about the people you spend time with and the activities you engage in. Select interactions that bring joy, inspiration, or learning, rather than those that leave you feeling depleted. This means saying yes to gatherings that align with your interests and values and gently declining those that don't. By prioritizing meaningful connections, you create a social life that supports your well-being rather than one driven by obligation or expectation. Mindful socialization fosters more profound relationships, where authenticity and mutual respect are at the core, enriching your life with genuine companionship.

The fear of being alone can be a significant barrier to embracing solitude. This anxiety often stems from the misconception that solitude equates to loneliness or inadequacy. However, by reframing solitude as a tool for resilience, you can begin to see its true value. Solitude offers a sanctuary where you can process emotions, recharge, and gain perspective. It empowers you to stand confidently in your own company, knowing that you are whole and complete just as you are; knowing that you like yourself just as you are now. Embracing solitude allows you to build resilience, equipping you with the strength to face life's challenges with grace and composure. It's in these moments of quiet reflection that you can cultivate inner peace, knowing that solitude is not a void but a canvas for self-expression and growth.

As I reflect on the balance between solitude and socialization, I realize that both are crucial to a fulfilling life. Solitude offers the opportunity for introspection and personal growth, while socialization brings joy, connection, and shared experiences. Together, they create a harmonious rhythm, each enhancing the other. By embracing solitude, you gain the self-awareness needed to engage with others meaningfully. And through mindful socialization, you enrich your life with relationships that support and inspire you. Finding this balance is a personal journey, one that evolves with time and experience, leading to a life that is both deeply connected and authentically your own.

In closing this chapter, remember that building a supportive community involves not just external connections, but also an internal one with yourself. Solitude and socialization work hand in hand, creating a balanced life filled with growth and connection. As we move forward, we will explore practical strategies for daily living, equipping you with the tools to navigate life's challenges with confidence and ease.

Chapter 5

Practical Strategies for Daily Living

There is a unique kind of solace in turning chaos into order, especially when the world feels unpredictable. Imagine waking up to a home that welcomes you with open arms, each room a sanctuary of calm rather than a reminder of tasks left undone. In the midst of life's upheavals, streamlining your household management can offer a comforting sense of control and peace. This chapter aims to guide you through practical strategies that transform your living space into a haven, offering both efficiency and tranquility. By optimizing organization, utilizing technology, and embracing collaboration, you can create a home that supports your well-being and nurtures resilience.

Decluttering is often the first step toward reclaiming control over your environment. Begin with simple tasks, like those suggested by the Sisterhood of Widows, to build motivation and gradually tackle more challenging areas. In the kitchen, remove dishes you rarely use and brighten the space with colorful dish towels. Painting cabinets white and using stackable bins in the pantry can create a sense of spaciousness and order. For personal spaces, consider a magazine holder to neatly store hair tools or tension rods to organize cutting boards. Keep a shopping bag in your closet for items you no longer need, ready to donate or discard. By organizing clothing by length and using clear shoeboxes, you'll create a wardrobe that's not only visually pleasing but also functional. Simplifying your book collection to those that truly spark interest can free up both physical and mental space. These decluttering techniques reduce chaos and empower you by fostering a sense of accomplishment and clarity.

I would like to suggest that, while decluttering, you have a place to store the things that you plan to discard for a short time. I have found that I am often too quick to discard items that I really need. This can be especially true of media cords, which I refer to as cat guts cluttering the room.

Efficient cleaning routines are another cornerstone of a well-managed home. Implementing daily checklists can help you maintain a tidy environment with minimal effort. Consider starting each day by making your bed, wiping down surfaces, and doing a quick sweep of high-traffic areas. These small tasks, when done consistently, prevent messes from piling up and make cleaning less daunting. Quick-clean strategies, like setting a timer for 15 minutes to tackle a specific area, can also be effective. Focus on high-impact areas like the kitchen or bathroom, where a little effort can make a big difference. By breaking tasks into manageable chunks, you create a rhythm of maintenance that keeps your home inviting and organized.

In our digital age, technology can be a powerful ally in household management. Smart home devices, such as automated lights or voice-activated assistants, can simplify daily tasks and enhance convenience. Imagine controlling the lights or thermostat with just a word or receiving reminders to water your plants or take out the trash. These small conveniences can save time and streamline your routine. Budgeting and inventory apps can also play a crucial role in managing household finances and supplies. Apps like Mint or Our Groceries help you track spending, plan meals, and keep an inventory of pantry staples, ensuring you always know what you have on hand. Embracing technology makes tasks more efficient and frees up mental space for what truly matters.

If you have children still at home, delegating tasks is equally important in maintaining a balanced and harmonious home. Sharing responsibilities with family not only lightens your load but also fosters a sense of teamwork and collaboration. Consider creating a family chore chart, assigning tasks based on age and ability. This chart can rotate weekly, ensuring everyone contributes to the household. If feasible, hiring cleaning services can also be a valuable investment. Professional cleaners can tackle deep-clean tasks, allowing you to focus on daily maintenance and other priorities. Remember, asking for help is a strength, not a weakness. It acknowledges that you don't have to do everything alone and that collaboration can lead to a more harmonious and balanced home life.

Interactive Element: Create Your Ideal Home Checklist

- **Declutter One Area:** Choose a specific room or space to start, like the kitchen or closet.

- **Daily Cleaning Tasks:** List three small cleaning tasks you can do each day.

- **Utilize Technology:** Identify one smart device or app to incorporate into your routine.

- **Delegate a Task:** Choose one household task to delegate to a family member or hire out.

By incorporating these strategies, you can transform your home into a space that nurtures and supports you, even amid life's challenges.

Simplifying Daily Routines

Imagine waking up each morning with a sense of calm, knowing exactly what the day holds. Designing a personalized daily schedule can create this sense of tranquility. Start by identifying your lifestyle and priorities. Morning rituals might include a quiet cup of tea, a few minutes of stretching, or a time of reflection as you read your Bible and pray. These rituals set a positive tone for the day, grounding you before the hustle begins. In the evening, consider activities that help you unwind, like reading or taking a warm bath. These bookends to your day create a comforting structure, providing consistency in a world that might feel unpredictable. Time-blocking techniques can add further efficiency to your schedule. By designating specific periods for tasks, you can focus on one activity at a time, reducing the chaos of multitasking. For example, allocate an hour in the morning for emails, a midday block for errands, and an afternoon slot for creative pursuits. This method allows you to fully engage in each moment.

Productivity techniques can transform how you approach tasks, making each day more fulfilling. The Pomodoro Technique, a time management method developed by Francesco Cirillo, encourages working in focused intervals. Set a timer for 25 minutes, dedicating yourself to a single task, then take a short break. This approach boosts concentration and prevents burnout. Prioritization matrices can also be invaluable. By categorizing tasks based on urgency and importance, you can tackle what's most critical first, ensuring that essential tasks don't get lost in the shuffle. This system helps you allocate your energy wisely, giving attention to what truly matters without becoming overwhelmed by less important duties. As you incorporate these techniques, you'll find that productivity doesn't mean doing more but achieving what you set out to do with purpose and clarity.

Balancing commitments with downtime is important in preventing burnout. It's easy to fill every moment with tasks, but scheduling breaks and leisure activities is just as important. Planned leisure activities, like a weekly movie night or a leisurely walk in the park, provide mental and emotional refreshment. These moments of joy offer a reprieve from daily demands, reminding you that life is to be savored, not just survived. Mindful relaxation periods, such as prayer, meditation, or deep breathing exercises, can also recharge your spirit. These practices invite you to pause, breathe, and refocus, easing stress and enhancing well-being. By deliberately carving out time for relaxation, you create a balance that sustains your energy and enthusiasm.

Life is inherently unpredictable, and maintaining flexibility in your routines can help you adapt to its ever-changing nature. While schedules provide structure, they should never become rigid constraints. Allow room for spontaneity and unexpected events. If a friend calls with an impromptu invitation, or if you feel the urge to take a detour during your daily walk, embrace these moments. Adjusting your schedule to accommodate such changes fosters resilience and adaptability. It reminds you that while routines are tools for organization, they should never hinder the joy of living in the present. Flexibility is about embracing life's surprises, finding beauty in the unexpected, and allowing your routine to evolve with you.

Decision-Making Confidence: Trusting Yourself

Navigating the maze of decision-making can often feel overwhelming, especially when life throws unexpected challenges our way. Understanding how decisions are made and the barriers that can hinder this process is crucial. Cognitive biases, those sneaky mental shortcuts, can cloud our judgment. They might lead us to give more weight to information that confirms our beliefs or make us overly confident in our choices. Then there's decision fatigue, the mental exhaustion that strikes after a day filled with choices, big and small. It can leave us feeling drained, making even simple decisions seem daunting. Recognizing these barriers is the first step toward reclaiming your decision-making power. It's about clearing the fog and seeing your choices with clarity and confidence, allowing you to act with assurance and purpose.

Developing a decision-making framework can serve as a reliable guide when you're faced with choices. Start with a pros and cons analysis, a straightforward method that helps weigh the positives and negatives of each option. Write them down, side by side, and consider not just the immediate impact but also the long-term consequences. This visual comparison can offer a clearer perspective, highlighting which choice aligns best with your goals and values. Decision trees and flowcharts can also be invaluable. They break down complex decisions into simpler steps, mapping out possible outcomes and paths. By following these visual aids, you can navigate through the decision-making process methodically, ensuring that each step is informed and deliberate.

Sometimes, though, the mind's logical analysis needs to be balanced with the heart's intuition. Encouraging intuitive decision-making means learning to trust that gut feeling, that inner voice that often knows what you need before you do. Intuition is not just a random impulse; it's a culmination of experiences and knowledge your subconscious has been gathering. To validate these gut feelings, pause and listen when they arise. Reflect on why you're drawn to a particular choice. Does it align with your core values and beliefs? Engaging in values alignment exercises can help. They prompt you to identify what matters most in your life, serving as a compass to guide your decisions. When your choices reflect your values, they feel right, resonating with a sense of authenticity and integrity.

Reflecting on past decisions can be immensely helpful in building confidence for the future. Look back at the choices you've made, both big and small. Analyze their outcomes: what worked, what didn't, and why. This reflection is not about self-criticism but about learning. Consider the decisions that led to positive outcomes. What patterns or strategies did you use? Likewise, examine those that didn't turn out as expected. What lessons did they offer? Learning from mistakes is a powerful teacher, providing insights that refine your decision-making skills over time. Each decision, regardless of its outcome, contributes to your growth, shaping you into someone who can make choices with wisdom and self-assurance. As you build this reflective practice, you deepen your understanding of yourself and your world, empowering you to face future decisions with renewed confidence.

Life Hacks for Stress-Free Living

Life often feels like a whirlwind, with tasks piling up faster than we can manage them. But there are practical tricks that can help ease this burden, allowing you more time for what truly matters. Meal prepping and batch cooking are lifesavers when it comes to simplifying your daily routine. I have a friend who spends just one afternoon preparing meals for the entire week. She chops vegetables, cooks grains, and portions them into containers, ready to grab and go. Not only does this save her time, but it also reduces the mental load of deciding what to cook each day. This practice brings with it the bonus of healthier eating, as you're less likely to resort to unhealthy takeout. Time-saving grocery shopping is another hack that streamlines your life. Craft a detailed list based on your meal plan and stick to it. This reduces time spent wandering aisles and limits impulse buys. Some find shopping online or using grocery delivery services a great way to avoid crowds and save precious minutes. These small changes can add significant ease to your life, turning what once felt like chores into manageable tasks.

Efficiency is about making life flow more smoothly. One key strategy is understanding when to multitask and when to focus on a single task. While multitasking can seem productive, it often divides attention and reduces effectiveness. Instead, consider strategic task grouping, which involves bundling similar tasks together. For example, tackle all your emails at once, then move on to phone calls, rather than jumping back and forth throughout the day. This approach minimizes the mental shift between different types of activities, making each more focused and efficient. When you concentrate on one thing at a time, you're more likely to complete it with quality and care.

Implementing this strategy can make a marked difference in your daily productivity, freeing up time and energy for other pursuits.

Minimalism offers a path to reduced stress and increased focus. It's about embracing simplicity and letting go of excess. Creating a capsule wardrobe is a practical step toward this lifestyle. Choose a limited number of versatile pieces that you love and feel confident wearing. This simplification makes dressing each day a breeze, eliminating the stress of decision-making and decluttering your closet. Minimalist home design follows similar principles. Consider open, airy spaces with fewer decorations and furniture. Each item should serve a purpose or bring joy. This approach not only makes your home more serene but also easier to maintain. With fewer distractions, you can focus more on experiences and relationships, which are the true treasures of life. Embracing minimalism isn't about deprivation; it's about finding richness in simplicity.

Creative problem-solving can be your ally in navigating life's challenges. Exploring unconventional solutions can lead to innovative ideas that streamline your day-to-day activities. DIY solutions for common problems are a fun and practical way to exercise creativity. For instance, if you need more storage, consider repurposing items you already own. An old ladder can become a charming bookshelf, or mason jars can organize your craft supplies. These projects solve problems and add a personal touch to your space. Innovative storage hacks, like using vertical space or hidden compartments, can maximize the usefulness of even the smallest areas. These solutions often require little more than imagination and a bit of elbow grease, yet they can transform how you interact with your environment. By looking at problems through a creative lens, you open yourself to a world of possibilities, making life not just easier but also more enjoyable.

Balancing Responsibilities and Self-Care

In the whirlwind of daily life, it's easy to lose sight of the crucial need for self-care amid a sea of responsibilities. Often, we prioritize tasks and obligations, leaving little room for ourselves. It's vital to acknowledge that self-care isn't a luxury but a necessity, much like breathing. Think of it as setting an appointment with yourself that you cannot miss. Begin by scheduling specific times in your day for activities that nurture your body and mind. These moments might include a brisk walk in the morning, a quiet tea break in the afternoon, or a time of prayer before bed. By integrating these into your routine, you create a buffer against stress and fatigue, allowing you to approach your responsibilities with renewed vigor.

Recognizing personal self-care needs is a deeply individual process. What rejuvenates one person might not work for another. Some find solace in the pages of a novel, while others might prefer the rhythm of a Zumba class. To uncover what truly nourishes you, consider taking a self-care assessment quiz. These quizzes can help pinpoint activities that resonate with you, offering a personalized roadmap to self-renewal. Once you've identified your preferences, weave them into your daily life. Embrace the activities that make your heart sing, whether it's a warm bath with your favorite scents or a quiet moment of reflection at dawn. These practices are not mere indulgences; they are foundations of well-being.

Setting boundaries is crucial in preserving your energy and time. It's easy to get caught in the web of commitments, stretching yourself too thin. Start by learning to say no gracefully. This doesn't mean shutting doors but rather choosing which ones to open. Declining additional responsibilities doesn't reflect selfishness but self-awareness. Set limits on work and social commitments to protect your personal time. Consider it a form of self-respect, acknowledging your limits and honoring them. Boundaries act as a shield, guarding your well-being against the relentless demands of the world. They allow you to focus on what's truly important, letting you engage fully in the moments that matter.

A self-compassionate mindset can transform how you view yourself and your place in the world. It's about treating yourself with the same kindness and understanding you would offer a dear friend. Self-compassion exercises can be simple yet profound. Try standing before a mirror, speaking words of kindness to your reflection. Affirmations for self-kindness, like "I am worthy" or "I am doing my best," can shift your internal dialogue from criticism to care. These affirmations, when repeated daily, can nurture a gentle acceptance of your human imperfections. Self-compassion is not just about being kind to yourself in success but embracing yourself in moments of struggle and doubt.

As life swirls around you with its demands and duties, remember that self-care is your anchor. Prioritizing it alongside responsibilities isn't a matter of selfishness but of sustainability. By scheduling self-care, setting boundaries, and cultivating self-compassion, you create a life that supports both your outer obligations and inner needs. This balance is not a static achievement but a dynamic practice, adapting to the ebbs and flows of life.

Creating Personal Rituals for Stability

In times of transition, when life feels like it's spinning out of control, personal rituals can provide much-needed structure and comfort. These rituals act as anchors, grounding you in the familiar when everything else seems uncertain. Morning rituals, for instance, can set a calming tone for the day ahead. Whether it's a few moments of meditation, sipping a cup of warm coffee while watching the sunrise, or a gentle stretch to awaken your body, these small acts can create a sense of peace and readiness. They are simple yet powerful ways to claim the day as your own, giving you a moment to breathe and prepare for what lies ahead. As the sun sets, evening reflection practices can offer a space for unwinding. Consider ending your day with a quiet reflection, jotting down thoughts or gratitude in a journal, or simply spending a few minutes in silence, letting the events of the day settle. These practices can help you release the day's tensions, making way for a restful night.

Creating personal rituals that resonate deeply with your values and needs is an intimate process. Start by reflecting on what truly matters to you. Is it family, creativity, or perhaps personal growth? Crafting personalized affirmations can be a starting point. These are simple, positive statements that embody your values and aspirations. Write them down and place them where you can see them daily, such as on your bathroom mirror or beside your bed. They serve as gentle reminders of your intentions and can focus your mind on what you want to cultivate in your life. Designing a gratitude practice can further enrich your ritual repertoire. Take a moment each day to note down at least three things you're grateful for. This practice shifts your focus from what's lacking to the abundance that still exists, fostering a sense of contentment and appreciation. The beauty of these rituals lies in their personalization; they are reflections of who you are and what you hold dear.

Incorporating these rituals into your daily routine requires intention. It's about finding ways to weave them into the fabric of your day so they become natural and seamless. Consider using ritual reminders and cues to help you stay consistent. Set alarms on your phone, use sticky notes, or create visual prompts that signal when it's time for a ritual. For example, a favorite song can cue your morning meditation, or the smell of a particular candle might signal your evening reflection time. These cues help you transition smoothly between daily activities, reinforcing the presence of your rituals in your life. They are gentle nudges that remind you to pause and engage with your practices, ensuring they remain a consistent source of support.

Just as life changes, so too should your rituals. Periodically reviewing and adjusting them ensures they continue to serve you well. Create a ritual evaluation checklist to assess their relevance and impact. Reflect on each ritual: Does it still resonate with your values? Does it bring you joy or peace? If a ritual feels stale or burdensome, consider modifying it or replacing it with something new. This flexibility keeps your rituals dynamic and aligned with your evolving self. Regularly assessing your practices ensures they remain meaningful and effective, preventing them from becoming mere habits without purpose. It's about maintaining a living connection with your rituals, allowing them to grow and change alongside you. This ongoing refinement keeps them fresh and impactful, ensuring they continue to nurture and support you through life's ebbs and flows.

As we conclude this chapter, remember that personal rituals are your sanctuary, providing stability and comfort amid change. They are deeply personal, reflecting your unique journey and aspirations. As you cultivate these rituals, you'll find they enrich your life, offering moments of peace and reflection in the midst of chaos. They are the threads that weave continuity and meaning into your days, reminding you of who you are and what you hold dear. These rituals, simple yet profound, are your allies in creating a life of balance and fulfillment. As we move forward, we'll explore how to embrace new possibilities, opening doors to growth and transformation.

Chapter 6

Embracing New Possibilities

The sun rises each day with a promise of new beginnings, a gentle reminder that life continues to unfold, even in the shadow of loss. I like to remember that God said in the Bible that "His mercies are new every morning." Widowhood, for many, can feel like an endless winter, each day blending into the next with a chill that seems inescapable. Yet, within this season of stillness lies the seed of renewal, waiting for the warmth of hope to coax it into bloom. Embracing new possibilities is about nurturing this seed, allowing it to grow and flourish amid the complexities of grief. It is about recognizing that even as we hold our past close, there is a future rich with potential and promise. This chapter invites you to explore the art of letting go, an essential practice in moving forward with grace and intention.

Letting go doesn't mean forgetting; it is about releasing the grip of the past to make space for the present. Holding on to past experiences, especially those marked by loss and heartache, can create a heaviness that confines us. This weight can stifle growth and obscure the possibilities that lie ahead. Releasing these attachments is crucial for personal growth, allowing you to step into a space where new opportunities can take root. Emotional release techniques, such as crying, praying, or breath meditation, can be powerful tools in this process. Crying, as mentioned in Source 1, is a natural response that can improve brain chemistry by releasing endorphins and reducing stress hormones. Praying reinforces the fact that you are never really alone. Breath meditation, where you visualize exhaling grief as a dark fog and inhaling love and light, can lighten the heart, offering a moment of peace and renewal.

Acceptance is the gentle art of acknowledging your past without letting it define you. It is an invitation to embrace your experiences as part of your life story, without judgment or regret. Acceptance serves as a form of healing, transforming wounds into wisdom. By accepting what has been, you free yourself from the constraints of what could have been, opening the door to what can be. Visualization exercises can aid in this process, helping you envision a future unburdened by past sorrows. Picture yourself surrounded by light, each breath drawing you further away from the shadows of yesterday. As you embrace this vision, you cultivate a sense of peace and clarity, empowering you to step forward with confidence.

Moving forward requires more than just intention; it calls for action that honors both the past and the future. Creating a symbolic goodbye ritual can offer closure, helping to signify the transition from holding on to moving forward. This ritual might involve writing a letter to your lost loved one, expressing gratitude for the shared moments, and releasing any lingering regrets. Burn or bury this letter as a symbolic act of letting go, transforming it into a gesture of peace and resolution. Such rituals, deeply personal yet profoundly healing, provide a tangible way to release the past and embrace the future. Additionally, writing a letter of closure to yourself can be a powerful exercise, allowing you to articulate your hopes and intentions for the days ahead.

The benefits of moving on are manifold, touching every aspect of your being. As you release the ties that bind you to the past, you create space for increased mental clarity. This newfound clarity sharpens your focus, enabling you to see possibilities where once there were only obstacles. Letting go also enhances emotional resilience, fortifying your spirit against future challenges. With each step forward, you build a reservoir of strength, drawn from the depths of your experiences. This resilience becomes a foundation upon which you can construct a life that honors the past while celebrating the present.

Interactive Element: Visualization Exercise

Sit in a quiet space, close your eyes, and take a deep breath. Visualize a path before you, lined with the memories of your past. As you walk, imagine these memories gently falling away, leaving room for the sunlight of new possibilities to guide your way. Allow this path to lead you to a place of peace and acceptance, where the weight of the past no longer holds sway. With each breath, feel the lightness of your spirit, free and unencumbered, ready to embrace the future with open arms.

Exploring New Hobbies and Interests

Imagine waking up one morning and deciding to try something completely foreign to you, like enrolling in a dance class. The idea might seem daunting at first, but it carries the promise of transformation. Stepping onto the dance floor for the first time, you might feel a mix of excitement and nerves. As the music begins, you find yourself moving to the rhythm, your body learning to express itself in new ways. Each step, each movement, becomes a testament to your willingness to embrace the unfamiliar. Dance isn't just about the physical; it's about letting go of fears and embracing newfound freedom. This experience can be both liberating and exhilarating, breathing new life into your spirit.

Learning a musical instrument offers another avenue for discovery. Picture yourself seated at a piano, your fingers tentatively pressing the keys. At first, the notes may sound disjointed, but with practice, they start to form melodies. As you immerse yourself in the music, the world around you fades away, leaving only you and the sound. Playing an instrument challenges your mind and body, enhancing cognitive skills and unlocking creativity. You might find yourself lost in the music, the rhythm and harmony weaving a tapestry of sound that speaks to your soul. This endeavor can become a cherished ritual, a time to connect with yourself and the beauty of creation.

The benefits of exploring new hobbies extend far beyond the immediate pleasure they bring. Engaging in activities that stimulate the mind and body can significantly improve mental health, offering a sense of accomplishment and well-being. Creativity blossoms as you learn to explore unconventional solutions, finding innovative answers to challenges. Cognitive skills sharpen as new neural pathways form with each new piece of knowledge or skill acquired. This mental exercise can ward off the monotony of routine, reinvigorating your daily life with a fresh perspective. The satisfaction of seeing progress, no matter how small, fuels a sense of pride and self-worth, affirming your ability to learn and grow.

In the realm of hobbies, the possibilities are boundless. Gardening, for instance, can provide relaxation and a connection to nature. The act of tending plants, watching them grow and flourish under your care, brings a sense of calm and fulfillment. Photography offers another creative outlet, allowing you to capture the world through your unique lens. Each photo becomes a story, a captured moment, expressing your view of the world. Whether it's the vibrant colors of a sunset or the intricate details of a flower, photography invites you to explore the beauty that surrounds you.

Consider the story of Sarah, a widow who discovered a passion for painting. Initially seeking a distraction, Sarah found herself drawn to the canvas, where she could express emotions that words could not capture. Each brushstroke became a conversation with herself, a way to process grief and find joy in the creation of something beautiful. Her paintings, once a private solace, now hang in galleries, sharing her journey with others. Through art, Sarah found a new purpose, a way to connect with others and honor her experiences. Her story illustrates the profound impact that exploring new hobbies can have, opening doors to unexpected paths and new beginnings.

Traveling Solo: Adventures and Insights

Traveling alone can be a powerful declaration of independence, especially when life has recently changed shape. When you set off on a solo adventure, you are not just exploring new places; you are charting new territory within yourself. The act of navigating a foreign city or a quiet countryside alone builds self-reliance like nothing else. You learn to trust your instincts, make decisions on the fly, and find comfort in your own company. Each step you take reinforces the belief that you are capable and that you can handle whatever comes your way. The confidence gained from solo travel often spills over into other areas of life, reinforcing your ability to stand strong on your own.

To ensure your solo travels are both safe and enjoyable, a bit of preparation goes a long way. Start by researching your destination thoroughly. Learn about the culture, the language, and the local customs. Understanding these aspects not only enriches your experience but also helps you blend in better and avoid misunderstandings. Choose accommodations that are known for being safe and welcoming to solo travelers. Read reviews, check ratings, and perhaps even reach out to other solo travelers for recommendations. Packing is another crucial step. Keep it light, focusing on essentials like comfortable shoes, a versatile wardrobe, and a reliable travel guide. Please remember to pack a small first-aid kit just in case. These preparations can make your journey smoother and more enjoyable.

Certain destinations stand out as particularly welcoming to those traveling alone. Cities with strong public transportation systems, like Tokyo or Amsterdam, make it easy to explore without a car, offering freedom and flexibility. These cities often have vibrant cultures and an array of activities, ensuring you'll never run out of things to do. Consider joining local tours or activities specifically geared toward solo travelers. This is not only a fantastic way to see the sights but also an opportunity to meet fellow adventurers. You can share stories, tips, and perhaps even form friendships that last beyond the trip. The community you find on the road can become an integral part of your travel experience, enriching each moment with shared excitement and understanding.

Personal stories of solo travel success abound, each one a testament to the transformative power of setting out alone. Take, for example, Jane, who decided to visit a national park by herself. Initially apprehensive, she quickly found solace in the natural beauty surrounding her. Hiking through trails, she felt a profound connection to the world and to herself. Each step on the path was a meditation, a silent conversation with her thoughts. The solitude allowed her to reflect, to let go of past burdens, and to embrace the present with an open heart. By the end of her trip, Jane had not only explored the park but had also discovered a well of inner strength she hadn't realized was there. Her journey became a turning point, a reminder that she could create her own adventures and find joy in the unexpected.

Consider the empowering act of traveling solo to redefine yourself, to step outside familiar boundaries, and to embrace the unknown. It's a chance to learn who you are when the world is your only companion. The empowerment that comes from navigating new cities and cultures on your own terms is a gift that keeps giving long after the trip is over. With each solo journey, you build a narrative of resilience and independence, a story that is uniquely your own. This exploration is not just about the places you visit; it is about the person you become along the way.

Setting New Life Goals and Dreams

What would life look like without limits? Take a moment to imagine it. This act of envisioning your future is the first step toward setting new life goals and dreams. It's about allowing yourself the freedom to dream, to explore what truly ignites your passion, and to pursue it with vigor. As you contemplate this, consider creating a vision board. Gather images, words, and symbols that speak to your heart and arrange them where you can see them daily. This collage becomes a visual representation of your aspirations, a constant reminder of what you are working toward. It serves as a compass, guiding you through the myriad of possibilities life offers, keeping your dreams vivid and within reach.

To transform these dreams into reality, structured goal-setting techniques are indispensable. Begin with visualization techniques, where you see your goals and feel them, as if they are already part of your life. Close your eyes and imagine the details: the sounds, the smells, the emotions tied to achieving your goals. This practice not only solidifies your aspirations but also fuels your motivation to act. Reverse engineering long-term goals is another effective strategy. Start with your end goal in mind and work backward, identifying the steps needed to get there. This method breaks down seemingly daunting tasks into manageable actions, making the path to success clearer and more attainable.

Dreaming big is a bold act of defiance against the constraints of fear and doubt. It's about believing in possibilities beyond the immediate horizon and daring to pursue them. It's about asking, "What would I do if I knew I couldn't fail?" These dreams are not just idle fantasies; they are the seeds of future realities. They challenge us to push boundaries and redefine our potential. Embrace the audacity to dream without limitations, for within these dreams lies the power to transform your life in ways you may never have imagined. By allowing yourself to dream expansively, you open the door to a world of opportunities and experiences that can enrich your life immeasurably.

Consider the story of Emma, who, after losing her partner, found herself at a crossroads. Faced with the challenge of redefining her life, she decided to pursue a long-held dream of starting her own business. Emma had always been passionate about baking, a hobby she shared with her late husband. Turning this passion into a livelihood seemed both daunting and exhilarating. With determination, she began by selling her baked goods at local markets. The response was overwhelmingly positive, fueling her confidence and expanding her ambitions. Despite the odds, Emma's business flourished, becoming a beloved staple in her community. Her story is a testament to the power of dreams, illustrating how they can be catalysts for change and growth. Emma's journey from loss to success exemplifies how setting life goals and pursuing them with passion can create new beginnings, filled with purpose and joy.

As you think about setting your life goals, remember that it's not about the destination, but the courage to take the first step. It's about trusting in your ability to bring your dreams to life and taking deliberate actions to make them happen. Whether your dream is to start a business, travel the world, or learn a new skill, each goal is a stepping stone on the path to a richer, more fulfilling life. Embrace the journey with open arms and a willing heart, for the possibilities are as vast as your imagination allows.

Embracing Change with an Open Heart

Life is a tapestry woven with threads of change, each one adding depth and color to our existence. Change, in its many forms, is inevitable, touching every corner of our lives. It arrives quietly at times, like the gentle turning of seasons, or with the sudden intensity of a summer storm. While it can be unsettling, change holds the promise of new beginnings, acting as a catalyst for personal growth. Embracing this constant allows us to navigate life's transitions with positivity and grace. By viewing change not as a disruption but as an opportunity for evolution, we open ourselves to the growth it brings, nurturing resilience along the way. This perspective transforms change from an adversary into an ally, guiding us toward a future rich with potential and promise.

Adapting to change requires more than acceptance; it calls for a shift in mindset that encourages openness and flexibility. One effective technique for fostering adaptability is to practice mindset shifts that embrace change as a natural part of life. Start by reframing your thoughts, viewing change not as a loss but as a chance to learn and grow. Consider each new situation an opportunity to develop new skills or explore new interests. Flexibility exercises in daily life can further enhance your ability to adapt. These exercises might include trying out different routines, experimenting with new approaches to familiar tasks, or engaging in activities that challenge your comfort zone. By incorporating these practices into your daily life, you cultivate a mindset that welcomes change, viewing it as a door to new possibilities.

An open heart invites the unexpected into our lives, allowing us to embrace change with curiosity rather than fear. This openness can lead to unexpected opportunities, such as new friendships and experiences that enrich our lives. By remaining receptive to the world around us, we create space for serendipity to work its magic, introducing us to people and places that broaden our horizons. Each encounter, whether planned or spontaneous, becomes a thread in the tapestry of our lives, adding richness and depth to our experiences. This openness fosters a sense of connection to the world, reminding us that we are part of a larger story, one that is constantly unfolding and evolving.

Fostering a mindset of curiosity and exploration is key to embracing change with an open heart. Approach life with a sense of wonder, viewing each day as an adventure waiting to be discovered. Try new foods, savoring the flavors and aromas that transport you to far-off lands. Immerse yourself in new cultures, allowing their customs and traditions to expand your understanding of the world. By stepping outside your comfort zone, you invite growth and transformation into your life. This adventurous spirit enriches your experiences and strengthens your resilience, equipping you to face future changes with confidence and grace. Curiosity becomes a guiding light, illuminating the path to personal growth and fulfillment.

As you navigate the ever-changing landscape of life, remember that change is not a destination but a journey. It is a continuous process of discovery and growth, inviting us to explore the depths of our potential. With an open heart and a curious mind, we can embrace change as a source of inspiration and empowerment, transforming challenges into opportunities for personal evolution. Each step forward becomes a testament to our resilience and adaptability, reminding us that we are capable of creating a life that is rich in meaning and possibility. As we embrace the dance of change, we open ourselves to a world of endless possibilities, each one waiting to be discovered and cherished.

Celebrating Small Wins on the Journey

In the tapestry of life, each small victory is a thread that weaves its way through the fabric of our existence, adding color and texture to our story. Recognizing these achievements, however modest they may seem, is vital to nurturing a sense of accomplishment and progress. It's easy to overlook the small wins as we focus on larger goals, but these moments of success are the building blocks of personal growth. By acknowledging them, you permit yourself to rejoice in your efforts and the strides you've made. Consider creating a "success jar," a simple yet powerful tool to capture these moments. Each time you achieve something, no matter how small, write it on a slip of paper and place it in the jar. Over time, this collection becomes a tangible reminder of your resilience and capability, a reservoir of positivity to draw from when the path ahead feels daunting.

The power of small wins lies in their ability to create momentum. Just as a single drop of water can set off ripples across a pond, each accomplishment fuels the next, propelling you forward on your path. This cumulative effect can lead to significant changes over time, as the confidence gained from one success encourages further action. By focusing on incremental progress, you build a foundation of self-assurance and motivation. These small steps, often taken in the face of uncertainty, become a testament to your determination and strength. They remind you that progress doesn't always require giant leaps; sometimes, it's the quiet persistence of putting one foot in front of the other that leads to transformation.

Celebrating achievements is an essential part of this process, providing a moment to pause and appreciate your journey. Treating yourself to a favorite activity can serve as a reward for your hard work, a way to honor your commitment and dedication. Whether it's indulging in a relaxing bath, enjoying a favorite meal, or taking time for a cherished hobby, these moments of self-care reinforce the value of your efforts. Sharing successes with friends and family can also amplify the joy of achievement. Their encouragement and pride in your accomplishments add layers of meaning to your triumphs, fostering a sense of community and connection. By celebrating together, you create shared memories that strengthen bonds and inspire collective growth.

To sustain motivation and perseverance, consider establishing a personal rewards system. This system doesn't have to be elaborate; it can be as simple as setting aside time for a leisurely walk after completing a challenging task or treating yourself to a movie night after reaching a milestone. The key is to align rewards with your personal preferences and values, ensuring they feel both meaningful and satisfying. This approach not only reinforces positive behavior but also cultivates a mindset that values progress and persistence. With each reward, you reaffirm your commitment to growth, fueling your determination to continue moving forward.

As we celebrate these small victories, let us recognize their role in shaping our lives. Each success, no matter how small, contributes to the larger picture of who we are becoming. These moments of achievement remind us of our capacity for growth and resilience, encouraging us to embrace the journey with an open heart and a determined spirit. As we look ahead, let these victories inspire us to face the challenges of tomorrow with courage and optimism, knowing that every step we take brings us closer to the life we envision.

In acknowledging our progress, we see the way toward a future filled with possibility and promise. As we move forward, we continue to build upon these foundations, creating a life rich with experiences and triumphs that reflect our deepest aspirations and dreams.

Chapter 7

Navigating New Relationships

The first time I considered the possibility of dating again, it felt like stepping into an unfamiliar land. There was a mixture of curiosity and trepidation, like walking through a door that had long remained closed. The world of new relationships after loss can be intimidating, filled with uncertainties and questions that linger in the mind. Am I ready to open my heart to someone new? How do I honor my past while embracing what lies ahead? These questions are both universal and deeply personal. They resonate with anyone who has loved and lost, and they form the foundation of exploring new beginnings.

Understanding your readiness for a new relationship begins with self-reflection. It's important to pause and consider your emotional state. This is not a decision to be rushed, but rather one that requires thoughtful introspection. Engaging in self-reflection exercises can help clarify your feelings and intentions. Take a moment to sit quietly, perhaps with a journal in hand, and ask yourself: What do I truly want from a new relationship? Am I seeking companionship, intimacy, or simply someone to share life's moments with? Journaling can be a powerful tool in this process, allowing you to articulate your desires and fears. Through writing, you may discover insights that guide your journey forward.

As you reflect, consider taking an "Am I Ready?" self-assessment quiz. This exercise can serve as a gentle guide, prompting you to evaluate your emotional readiness. Questions might include: Have I allowed myself time to grieve? Do I feel excited about meeting new people? Am I prepared to accept someone for who they are, without comparisons to my past partner? These reflections can help illuminate your current mindset, offering clarity on whether you are ready to embark on a new chapter. The answers aren't definitive, but they provide a starting point for understanding your readiness.

It's also essential to identify any emotional barriers that may hinder your ability to move forward. Fear of vulnerability is a common obstacle, as opening up to someone new can feel daunting. You may worry about the possibility of being hurt again or fear the unknowns that accompany new relationships. Remnants of past guilt might linger as well, whispering that moving on is a betrayal of your past love. Recognizing these barriers is the first step in overcoming them. By acknowledging their presence, you can begin to work through them, gradually dismantling the walls that stand between you and new possibilities.

Self-awareness is key in this journey. Understanding your emotional state is crucial before entering new relationships. It allows you to approach potential connections with honesty and clarity, setting the stage for healthy interactions. Self-awareness fosters a deeper connection to your own needs and desires, enabling you to communicate them effectively to others. It also empowers you to recognize when you're truly ready to embrace a new relationship, rather than acting out of loneliness or societal pressure. This awareness is a gift, offering you the foundation to build meaningful relationships that honor both your past and your future.

For me, I know that I always compare any new person in the light of my lost husband, and no one can measure up. I know that this isn't fair to the other person, but I also know myself, and until I can get beyond this hurdle, I won't move forward with a new relationship. I am determined to clear this hurdle, and I know that with time, God willing, I will overcome this challenge. However, to be fair, we must always be self-aware.

Signs of readiness for dating again can be subtle, yet significant. Feeling excited about socializing and meeting new people is a positive indicator. It suggests a willingness to explore the world beyond the confines of loss. Emotional stability and balance are also crucial. If you find that your grief no longer consumes you and you can experience joy without guilt, it may be time to consider new relationships. These signs are not definitive markers, but rather gentle nudges that signal your heart's openness to new experiences. Embracing these indicators with an open mind and heart can lead to fulfilling connections that enrich your life in unexpected ways.

Understanding your readiness for a new relationship begins with self-reflection. It's important to pause and consider your emotional state. This is not a decision to be rushed, but rather one that requires thoughtful introspection. Engaging in self-reflection exercises can help clarify your feelings and intentions. Take a moment to sit quietly, perhaps with a journal in hand, and ask yourself: What do I truly want from a new relationship? Am I seeking companionship, intimacy, or simply someone to share life's moments with? Journaling can be a powerful tool in this process, allowing you to articulate your desires and fears. Through writing, you may discover insights that guide your journey forward.

As you reflect, consider taking an "Am I Ready?" self-assessment quiz. This exercise can serve as a gentle guide, prompting you to evaluate your emotional readiness. Questions might include: Have I allowed myself time to grieve? Do I feel excited about meeting new people? Am I prepared to accept someone for who they are, without comparisons to my past partner? These reflections can help illuminate your current mindset, offering clarity on whether you are ready to embark on a new chapter. The answers aren't definitive, but they provide a starting point for understanding your readiness.

It's also essential to identify any emotional barriers that may hinder your ability to move forward. Fear of vulnerability is a common obstacle, as opening up to someone new can feel daunting. You may worry about the possibility of being hurt again or fear the unknowns that accompany new relationships. Remnants of past guilt might linger as well, whispering that moving on is a betrayal of your past love. Recognizing these barriers is the first step in overcoming them. By acknowledging their presence, you can begin to work through them, gradually dismantling the walls that stand between you and new possibilities.

Self-awareness is key in this journey. Understanding your emotional state is crucial before entering new relationships. It allows you to approach potential connections with honesty and clarity, setting the stage for healthy interactions. Self-awareness fosters a deeper connection to your own needs and desires, enabling you to communicate them effectively to others. It also empowers you to recognize when you're truly ready to embrace a new relationship, rather than acting out of loneliness or societal pressure. This awareness is a gift, offering you the foundation to build meaningful relationships that honor both your past and your future.

For me, I know that I always compare any new person in the light of my lost husband, and no one can measure up. I know that this isn't fair to the other person, but I also know myself, and until I can get beyond this hurdle, I won't move forward with a new relationship. I am determined to clear this hurdle, and I know that with time, God willing, I will overcome this challenge. However, to be fair, we must always be self-aware.

Signs of readiness for dating again can be subtle, yet significant. Feeling excited about socializing and meeting new people is a positive indicator. It suggests a willingness to explore the world beyond the confines of loss. Emotional stability and balance are also crucial. If you find that your grief no longer consumes you, and you can experience joy without guilt, it may be time to consider new relationships. These signs are not definitive markers, but rather gentle nudges that signal your heart's openness to new experiences. Embracing these indicators with an open mind and heart can lead to fulfilling connections that enrich your life in unexpected ways.

Interactive Element: "Am I Ready?" Self-Assessment Quiz

Take a moment to answer these questions honestly. They are meant to guide your reflection on emotional readiness for new relationships:

1. Have I allowed myself sufficient time to grieve and heal?

2. Do I feel excited or curious about meeting new people?

3. Am I able to think about my past partner without overwhelming sadness?

4. Can I envision a future that includes companionship and joy?

5. Am I prepared to accept someone new without comparing them to my past love?

Reflect on your responses and consider discussing them with a trusted friend or counselor for further insight.

Overcoming the Guilt of Moving On

Guilt often lingers in the shadows when considering the prospect of new relationships after loss. It can be an uninvited companion, whispering doubts and stirring internal conflicts. You might find yourself questioning, "Is it too soon?" or "Am I dishonoring my past love?" Such self-doubt is natural and shared by many who have walked this path. These feelings of guilt can weigh heavily, fostering an internal dialogue that is both relentless and exhausting. It's crucial to acknowledge these emotions without judgment, to validate them as part of the complex tapestry of grief and healing. Recognizing that guilt is a common response can provide some comfort, allowing you to see that you are not alone in experiencing this emotional turmoil.

The roots of guilt often extend deep into societal expectations and personal beliefs. Society sometimes imposes unspoken rules about how long one should grieve and when it is "appropriate" to move forward. These norms can create an invisible pressure, suggesting that moving on is a betrayal of your past. Similarly, personal values and beliefs can play a significant role. You may hold on to the idea that true love is eternal and that opening your heart to someone new diminishes the love you once shared. It's important to understand that these sources of guilt are not always rational, but they feel real and deserving of exploration. By examining these influences, you might begin to untangle the web of emotions that guilt creates, gaining clarity and perspective on your path forward.

Processing guilt is a gradual journey, one that benefits from intentional strategies. Consider engaging in guilt-reduction meditation, a practice that cultivates self-compassion and acceptance. In a quiet space, close your eyes and focus on your breath. With each inhale, invite compassion into your heart, and with each exhale, release the guilt that binds you. This practice can create a space of peace within, allowing you to confront guilt with kindness and understanding. Reframing your thoughts and perspectives is another powerful tool. Instead of viewing new relationships as a betrayal, consider them a testament to your capacity for love. Recognize that loving again does not erase the past; it honors it by allowing you to carry its lessons forward. As you shift your perspective, you may find that guilt begins to loosen its grip, replaced by a gentle acceptance of your evolving journey.

It's equally important to reassure yourself that moving on is a normal and healthy part of life's progression. Love is not a finite resource; it expands and transforms, adapting to the changing contours of your life. Embracing new relationships is a testament to resilience, a celebration of life's capacity for renewal. Consider the stories of others who have successfully navigated this transition. There are countless narratives of individuals who, after loss, found joy and companionship anew. These stories serve as gentle reminders that happiness and healing are possible, that opening your heart to new experiences does not mean closing the door on the past. They illustrate the beautiful complexity of love, one that is capable of holding both cherished memories and hopeful futures.

In the quiet moments of reflection, remember that guilt is but one of many emotions that accompany loss and renewal. It is a sign of love's enduring presence, a reminder of the connections that shape our lives. As you navigate the waters of new beginnings, allow yourself the grace to feel, to question, and to grow. Embrace the possibility of happiness with an open heart, knowing that each step forward is a tribute to the love that has guided you here.

Dating Again: Setting Boundaries and Expectations

When stepping into the realm of new relationships, setting personal boundaries becomes a fundamental act of self-care. Boundaries are not barriers; they are guidelines that define what is acceptable and what is not. They empower you to protect your emotional well-being while fostering healthy interactions. Identifying your non-negotiable factors is a crucial first step. These are the values and limits that you hold dear, the aspects of your life you are unwilling to compromise. Whether it's your need for personal space, the time you dedicate to family, or certain lifestyle choices, knowing these boundaries helps you communicate them clearly to a new partner. Early communication of these boundaries is vital. It sets the tone for mutual respect and understanding, ensuring that both parties are aware of each other's needs and limitations from the outset. This transparency can prevent misunderstandings and build a foundation of trust, creating a safe space for the relationship to flourish.

Realistic expectations are equally important when entering a new relationship. It's easy to be swept away by the excitement of new beginnings, but grounding yourself in reality paves the way for a more sustainable connection. Understand that every person, including yourself, comes with their own set of limitations. No partner will be perfect, and expecting them to fulfill every emotional need can lead to disappointment. Instead, focus on what truly matters to you. What qualities do you value in a partner? What are you willing to compromise on, and where do you draw the line? By reflecting on these questions, you can approach new relationships with a balanced perspective, appreciating your partner for who they are rather than an idealized version. This understanding fosters a healthier, more authentic connection.

Effective communication is the lifeblood of any relationship, particularly when navigating boundaries and expectations. Active listening is a skill worth cultivating. It involves not just hearing your partner's words, but truly understanding their meaning and intent. It means being present, giving your partner your full attention, and responding with empathy. When you listen actively, you create a space where open dialogue can thrive. Assertive communication techniques are also essential. Being assertive means expressing your needs and desires clearly and respectfully, without aggression or passivity. Practice using "I" statements, such as "I feel" or "I need," to convey your thoughts without sounding accusatory. This approach encourages honest exchanges and reinforces mutual respect. Remember, communication is a two-way street. Just as you express your needs, remain open to hearing and understanding your partner's perspective.

This reciprocal exchange strengthens the bond between you, laying the groundwork for a relationship built on mutual understanding.

Navigating potential challenges is an inevitable part of dating again. Differing relationship goals can arise, leading to confusion and conflict if not addressed. One partner may seek a casual connection, while the other desires something more committed. It's important to have candid conversations early on about what each of you wants from the relationship. Are you both seeking companionship, or is there a desire for something deeper? Discussing these goals openly allows you to assess compatibility and make informed decisions about the relationship's direction. Flexibility and compromise are key when differences arise. Approach these conversations with an open mind, acknowledging that each person's journey is unique. While some differences can be negotiated, others may be non-negotiable. It's crucial to recognize when a fundamental mismatch exists and to navigate these situations with honesty and compassion. By addressing challenges head-on and working together to find solutions, you pave the way for a resilient and fulfilling relationship.

Communicating with Family About New Relationships

In the landscape of new relationships, family communication becomes a cornerstone of building trust and understanding. Sharing news of a new relationship with family can feel daunting, but it is a vital step in maintaining openness. Family often holds shared memories and a deep connection to your past, making their involvement in your new chapter important. Telling them about your new relationship isn't just about keeping them informed; it's about inviting them into your evolving story. This openness can strengthen bonds, ensuring that your relationship with your family remains a source of support rather than tension. When family understands your intentions and emotions, they are more likely to respond with empathy and encouragement. This transparency fosters an environment where trust flourishes, laying the groundwork for a harmonious integration of new relationships into family life.

To facilitate these conversations, consider strategies that promote honest and respectful dialogue. Setting up a family meeting can provide a structured environment where everyone can express their thoughts and feelings. Choose a time and place where everyone feels comfortable and has the opportunity to participate. Begin the conversation by sharing your feelings and intentions openly. Express why this new relationship is important to you and how it contributes to your happiness and growth. Prepare for varied reactions, as family members may have different perspectives based on their own experiences and emotions. Some may react with enthusiasm, while others may need time to process the change. Be patient and willing to listen, allowing them to voice their thoughts without interruption. This approach respects their feelings and demonstrates your commitment to maintaining open lines of communication.

Anticipating family concerns is a proactive way to address potential objections with compassion and understanding. One common concern is the question of loyalty—whether moving on means forgetting or replacing the past. It's important to reassure your family that opening your heart to someone new does not diminish the love and memories you shared with your late partner. Instead, it honors those memories by allowing you to grow and find happiness again. Balancing family dynamics can be another challenge, especially if children are involved. They may have their own emotions and concerns about a new relationship. Engage them in the conversation, providing reassurance that your new relationship does not alter the love and attention you have for them. By addressing these concerns openly, you create a space for dialogue that acknowledges everyone's feelings and fosters mutual respect.

Family support plays a crucial role in nurturing new relationships. Their encouragement can provide a foundation of confidence and stability as you navigate this new chapter. Seeking their approval and advice can also strengthen your bond, showing that you value their perspective and wisdom. Involving them in your journey demonstrates that they remain an integral part of your life, even as you embrace new beginnings. Family can offer insights and guidance based on their own experiences, helping you navigate challenges with greater ease. Their support is a reminder that you are not alone, that you have a network of love and understanding to lean on. As you move forward, consider inviting them to meet your new partner, allowing them to build their own relationship. This gesture fosters connection and integration, reinforcing the idea that your new relationship is a welcome addition to the family tapestry, not a replacement of what once was.

Honoring Past Love While Embracing New Connections

Balancing the cherished memories of a past love while opening your heart to someone new is a delicate act, much like walking a tightrope. It involves honoring the love that once was without letting it overshadow the blossoming potential of new connections. This balance is not about forgetting the past but about integrating it into your present in a way that enriches both lives. Imagine your heart as a room filled with memories, each one a testament to the love you shared. These memories are yours to keep, to visit, and to celebrate, but they should not prevent you from inviting new experiences into your life.

One way to keep the memory of your past love alive is through respectful rituals that honor what you shared. Consider creating a memory box or scrapbook dedicated to your partner. Fill it with photographs, letters, and mementos that capture the essence of your time together. This tangible collection serves as a private sanctuary, a place where you can reminisce and feel connected to your past. Alternatively, you might choose to hold an annual remembrance ceremony on significant dates, such as anniversaries or birthdays. Lighting a candle, sharing stories with loved ones, or even spending a quiet moment in reflection can be powerful ways to honor your partner's memory while acknowledging the passage of time. These rituals provide a sense of continuity, allowing you to cherish your past while embracing the present.

Transparency with new partners is crucial in maintaining this balance. It's important to be open about your past love, sharing stories and memories that have shaped who you are today. These conversations need not be heavy or filled with sorrow; rather, they can be opportunities to celebrate the life you lived and the lessons you learned. By sharing these stories, you invite your new partner to understand the depth of your experiences, fostering a deeper connection built on honesty and mutual respect. This openness also sets the stage for your partner to share their own stories, creating a space where both pasts are acknowledged and valued. It's about building a relationship that respects what came before while looking toward the future with hope and excitement.

Each relationship you enter is a unique tapestry woven with threads of both differences and similarities. No two relationships are ever the same, and therein lies their beauty. Embrace the individuality of each connection, celebrating what makes them special. Perhaps your past partner shared your love for hiking, while your new partner introduces you to the joys of cooking. These differences enrich your life, offering new perspectives and experiences that broaden your horizons. At the same time, similarities can provide comfort and stability, reminding you of the qualities you value in companionship. Recognize that each relationship adds its own color and texture to the fabric of your life, contributing to a vibrant and diverse narrative that is uniquely yours.

In nurturing new connections, it's important to remember that love is not finite; it has the capacity to grow and adapt. By holding space for both past and present, you allow yourself the freedom to love fully and authentically. This balance is not about choosing one over the other but about creating a harmony that honors all parts of your heart. As you move forward, carry the wisdom of your past with you, letting it guide you in building relationships that are grounded in respect, understanding, and joy. In this way, you honor not only your past love but also the potential for new beginnings.

Finding Joy in Companionship and Love

As I sat across from my new partner, I realized how simple moments can bring unexpected joy. A shared meal, a walk in the park, or even a quiet evening watching television—these experiences weave a tapestry of companionship that enriches life. It is in these shared activities that happiness finds its way back, often unannounced. Companionship is not merely about having someone by your side; it is about the joy that comes from building memories together, no matter how small. Whether it's trying a new hobby, exploring a new place, or simply enjoying a cup of coffee in silence, these moments remind us of life's simple pleasures.

Companionship plays a profound role in emotional healing. New connections provide a unique support system, offering understanding and empathy that can soothe the heart. When you share your thoughts and feelings with someone who listens, it lightens the emotional load. Their presence can be a balm, helping to mend the wounds of loss. The understanding that comes from a partner who genuinely cares can bridge the gap between past pain and present healing. This emotional support fosters a sense of belonging and acceptance, allowing you to move forward with renewed strength. Love's gentle touch can transform sorrow into solace, making the journey less daunting.

Cultivating a mindset of gratitude and appreciation can further enhance the joy found in new relationships. Keeping a gratitude journal dedicated to your relationship encourages you to focus on the positive aspects. Each day, take a moment to jot down what you appreciate about your partner or the relationship. It might be their smile, a kind gesture, or a shared laugh. Reflecting on these moments fosters a sense of appreciation that deepens the connection. Gratitude shifts focus from what is lacking to what is thriving, nurturing a positive outlook that enriches the bond. In acknowledging the good, you cultivate an environment where love can flourish.

Confidence in the pursuit of love is vital. It is about approaching new relationships with hope and optimism, believing in the potential for happiness. Affirmations can be powerful allies on this path. Simple yet profound statements like "I am deserving of love" or "I welcome joy into my life" can bolster your confidence. These affirmations serve as reminders of your worthiness and potential for happiness. Stories of successful new beginnings can also inspire. Consider the tale of a widow who, after years of solitude, found companionship in an unexpected place. Her story is one of courage and renewal, illustrating that love can find you when you least expect it.

As you navigate new relationships, remember that each step forward is a testament to your resilience and capacity for love. Embrace the joy of companionship with an open heart, allowing it to bring color back into your life. The laughter shared, the support offered, and the gratitude felt all contribute to a rich tapestry of love and connection. You are not just surviving; you are thriving, discovering new aspects of yourself and your capacity for joy.

In embracing these connections, you set the stage for a life filled with love's possibilities. As we move into the next chapter, we will explore how to cultivate emotional and spiritual resilience, ensuring that your journey remains one of growth and fulfillment. Each step forward is a testament to your strength and a celebration of the life you continue to build.

Chapter 8

Cultivating Emotional and Spiritual Resilience

In the quiet moments of dawn, as the world slowly awakens, there's a serene stillness that invites reflection and presence. This gentle hour serves as a reminder of the power of the present moment, a concept deeply rooted in mindfulness. Mindfulness is a practice that encourages us to be fully present, to engage with our surroundings and our inner world without judgment. By fostering this awareness, we can build emotional resilience, a quality that allows us to recover from life's inevitable setbacks. This chapter explores how mindfulness can be a tool for strengthening your resilience, offering a sanctuary amid life's chaos.

Mindfulness meditation is a daily practice that can transform your approach to emotions and stress. It involves setting aside a few minutes each day to focus solely on your breath, observing each inhale and exhale with intention. This practice encourages a state of calm and clarity, helping you detach from the whirlwind of thoughts that often accompany grief and anxiety. As you breathe in, imagine drawing in peace and strength; as you breathe out, let go of tension and worry. Over time, this simple exercise can cultivate a deep sense of inner stability, allowing you to face challenges with greater equanimity and grace.

Alongside prayer, meditation, and mindful breathing techniques provide immediate relief in moments of stress. By consciously slowing your breath, you can activate the body's relaxation response, reducing the physiological effects of stress. This can be as simple as inhaling deeply through your nose, holding the breath for a few seconds, and then exhaling slowly through your mouth. This technique can be practiced anywhere, whether sitting quietly at home or amid a bustling day. It serves as a powerful reminder of your capacity to influence your state of mind through intentional, mindful actions.

Observing thoughts and feelings without judgment is a cornerstone of mindfulness. It encourages a gentle, compassionate awareness of your internal experiences, allowing you to view them with curiosity rather than criticism. Mindfulness also plays a significant role in stress reduction by enhancing emotional regulation and stability. Mindful walking exercises offer a practical way to integrate mindfulness into your routine. As you walk, pay attention to each step, the sensation of your feet touching the ground, and the rhythm of your breath. This simple activity anchors you in the present, reducing stress and promoting emotional balance. Walking mindfully is an opportunity to connect with your environment, noticing the beauty and subtleties that often go unnoticed in the rush of daily life.

Incorporating mindfulness into everyday activities can enrich your life with moments of peace and clarity. Mindful eating practices, for example, encourage you to savor each bite, appreciating the flavors, textures, and nourishment your food provides. This practice transforms a routine meal into a meditative experience, fostering gratitude and presence. Similarly, gratitude-focused mindfulness invites you to reflect on aspects of your life that bring joy and fulfillment, nurturing a positive outlook and resilience. By practicing gratitude, you train your mind to focus on abundance rather than lack, reinforcing a sense of contentment and peace.

Interactive Element: Mindful Moment Checklist

- **Mindful Breathing:** Set aside three minutes each morning to practice mindful breathing, focusing on each inhale and exhale

- **Mindful Walking:** Dedicate one walk per day to mindfulness, paying attention to each step and breath.

- **Mindful Eating:** Choose one meal per week to eat mindfully, savoring each bite and reflecting on the nourishment it provides.

- **Gratitude Practice:** Each evening, list three things you are grateful for, fostering a mindset of abundance and positivity.

By embracing these mindfulness practices, you unlock a reservoir of resilience and emotional stability. This chapter invites you to explore mindfulness as a path to inner peace, offering tools to navigate life's challenges with strength and serenity.

The Healing Power of Reflection and Journaling

Journaling offers a sanctuary for your thoughts, a private space where you can untangle emotions and gain clarity. Imagine sitting with a blank page and allowing your thoughts to flow freely, capturing whatever comes to mind. This is stream-of-consciousness writing, a technique that encourages you to write without restraint or judgment. It's not about crafting perfect sentences; it's about capturing the raw, unfiltered essence of your inner world. As your pen moves across the page, you may find that the act of writing helps to organize your thoughts, shedding light on feelings you might not have even realized were there. This practice can be particularly liberating, allowing you to explore the depths of your emotions without fear of criticism or misunderstanding.

In moments of emotional intensity, structured journaling exercises can provide relief. Emotion-focused free writing invites you to concentrate on a specific feeling or experience, writing continuously for a set period of time. Let the words spill onto the page, expressing anger, sadness, joy, or confusion without editing or censoring. Another powerful exercise involves writing a letter to your past self. This form of reflection can be profoundly healing, offering a chance to express compassion and understanding for the person you once were. It allows you to acknowledge the growth and resilience that have emerged from your experiences. These exercises serve as a release valve for pent-up emotions, providing a safe outlet for expression and insight.

Reflection through journaling is not only about emotional release; it is also a catalyst for personal growth. By engaging in reflective practices, you can gain valuable insights into your beliefs, behaviors, and patterns. Consider incorporating reflective question prompts into your journaling routine. Questions like "What did I learn today?" or "How did I overcome a challenge?" can guide your introspection, encouraging deeper understanding and self-awareness. End-of-day reflection exercises offer another opportunity for insight, prompting you to review your day and highlight moments of growth or gratitude. These practices foster self-discovery, helping you identify areas for development and celebrate progress.

Consistency is key to reaping the benefits of journaling. Establishing a regular habit can enhance the impact of your reflections, allowing for sustained growth and clarity. Set a journaling schedule that works for you, whether it involves writing daily, weekly, or whenever inspiration strikes. The important thing is to create a routine that becomes a natural part of your life. Consider choosing a specific time of day for your journaling practice, such as morning or evening, to help reinforce this habit. As you commit to regular journaling, you'll likely notice a gradual shift in your emotional well-being and personal insight. The act of putting pen to paper becomes a ritual of self-care, nurturing your mind and spirit through the power of reflection.

Interactive Element: Journaling Reflection Prompts

- **Daily Reflection Prompt:** "What am I grateful for today?"

- **Emotion-Focused Free Writing:** Choose one emotion and write about it for ten minutes.

- **Letter to Past Self:** Write a letter expressing gratitude and compassion for who you were.

- **End-of-Day Reflection:** "What did I learn about myself today?"

In cultivating this journaling practice, you create a space for healing and transformation. Through the written word, you explore the layers of your emotions, gaining clarity and insight that pave the way for growth and renewal.

Spiritual Practices for Inner Peace

There is a profound tranquility that accompanies spiritual practices, a soothing balm for the soul that craves solace and understanding. Yoga and meditation retreats offer a sanctuary away from the clamor of daily life, providing space to reconnect with the self. These retreats immerse you in an environment where the body and mind can find harmony through movement and stillness. Yoga, with its gentle stretches and poses, encourages a deep connection to your breath and body. Meditation, meanwhile, quiets the mind, opening the door to inner peace and clarity. Breathwork sessions, another powerful practice, focus on the rhythm of inhalation and exhalation, helping to release tension and cultivate calm. Each breath becomes a bridge to the present moment, anchoring you in a state of serenity.

Exploring your personal spirituality can be a deeply rewarding endeavor. It involves delving into beliefs and practices that resonate with your core values and experiences. Nature-based spirituality, for example, draws inspiration from the natural world, finding divinity in the rustling leaves, the flow of a river, or the vastness of the sky. Engaging with nature can ground you, offering a sense of belonging and perspective. Rituals and ceremonies, whether personal or communal, provide structure and meaning, marking significant moments or transitions with intention. These practices can be as simple as lighting a candle in remembrance or as elaborate as a seasonal celebration with friends. They serve as touchstones, connecting you to something greater than yourself and fostering a sense of continuity and purpose.

The impact of spirituality on well-being is profound. Spiritual practices enhance overall well-being by fostering a sense of connection, both to others and to the universe. Involvement in spiritual communities can provide support and companionship, offering a space where shared beliefs and values create a strong bond. Whether through a church, a meditation group, or a book club focused on spiritual texts, these communities offer a network of understanding and encouragement. They are places where you can share your spiritual journey and draw strength from the collective wisdom of others. This sense of community can be deeply comforting, reminding you that you are not alone in your quest for peace and meaning.

To deepen your spiritual journey, various resources are available to guide and inspire you. Spiritual literature offers insights and wisdom from diverse traditions and perspectives. Books like "The Power of Now" by Eckhart Tolle or "The Four Agreements" by Don Miguel Ruiz can provide guidance and provoke thoughtful reflection. Online spiritual communities, such as forums or virtual meditation groups, offer a platform to connect with others who share your interests and values. Websites like Mindful.org or Gaia.com offer resources ranging from articles to video courses, supporting your exploration of spiritual practices. These resources can be a source of inspiration and learning, enriching your understanding and practice of spirituality.

As you explore these spiritual practices, remember that the path to inner peace is deeply personal. It is a journey of discovery, where each practice and belief is a step toward greater understanding and tranquility. Embrace the exploration with an open heart, allowing your spirituality to unfold in its own time and way, bringing comfort and clarity to your life.

Embracing a Growth Mindset

Imagine seeing life's challenges not as obstacles but as stepping stones on the path of personal development. This perspective is the essence of a growth mindset. Unlike a fixed mindset, which sees abilities as static and unchangeable, a growth mindset embraces the idea that skills and intelligence can evolve with effort and perseverance. This shift in perspective can dramatically impact resilience, transforming setbacks into opportunities for learning and growth. When faced with difficulties, a person with a growth mindset asks, "What can I learn from this?" rather than dwelling on limitations. This approach fosters adaptability, turning each challenge into a chance to expand one's capabilities and knowledge.

Adopting a growth mindset involves viewing setbacks as valuable learning experiences. Instead of perceiving failure as a reflection of inadequacy, it becomes a narrative of resilience and progress. Reframing failure narratives is a powerful exercise in shifting perspective. Consider the setbacks you've faced in the past. Reflect on the lessons learned and how they contributed to your growth. This reflection helps rewire your mindset, allowing you to see challenges as integral to the growth process. By changing the narrative, you build a resilient spirit that welcomes new experiences with open arms, knowing that each one contributes to your personal evolution.

To cultivate a growth mindset, practical exercises can be incorporated into your daily routine. Affirmations for growth are a simple yet effective tool. By repeating positive statements such as "I am capable of learning" or "Challenges help me grow," you reinforce a mindset that embraces change and development. These affirmations can be written down and placed where you'll see them daily, serving as constant reminders of your potential. In addition, mindset journaling exercises can deepen your understanding of your thought patterns. Dedicate a few minutes each day to writing about a challenge you're facing. Explore your feelings, identify what you can learn, and set a goal for how you'll approach the situation differently next time. This practice not only fosters a growth mindset but also enhances self-awareness and problem-solving skills.

The benefits of adopting a growth mindset extend beyond overcoming challenges; it paves the way for increased adaptability and success in all areas of life. When you approach situations with the belief that effort leads to improvement, you become more open to taking risks and trying new things. This openness can lead to unexpected opportunities and achievements. Consider stories of individuals who have applied a growth mindset to their pursuits. Perhaps you've heard of someone who, despite initial setbacks, learned new skills and eventually excelled in a field they once found daunting. These success stories illustrate the transformative power of a growth mindset, showcasing how embracing challenges with courage and curiosity can unlock greater potential and fulfillment.

In embracing a growth mindset, you cultivate a resilience that empowers you to navigate life's uncertainties with confidence and determination. This mindset encourages continuous learning and personal development, turning each experience into a stepping stone toward success and self-discovery. As you integrate these practices into your life, you'll find that challenges become less daunting, and the possibilities for growth become limitless.

Finding Meaning and Purpose After Loss

In the midst of loss, the search for meaning can become a guiding force, illuminating paths that might otherwise remain hidden. Identifying what truly matters to you is an exercise in introspection, one that can reveal core values that define who you are and what you stand for. These values, whether they encompass compassion, creativity, or community, serve as anchors in turbulent times. They act as beacons, guiding you toward activities and choices that align with your deepest beliefs. Meaning-making activities, such as volunteering, engaging in creative pursuits, or mentoring others, can transform abstract values into concrete actions. Through these endeavors, you find purpose—a reason to rise each day, not merely to survive but to contribute and connect.

A profound sense of purpose can be a balm for the soul, offering direction and motivation when the road ahead feels uncertain. It can ease the weight of grief by shifting focus from what has been lost to what can still be gained. Purpose provides a framework for healing, encouraging you to envision a future where your experiences and insights become sources of strength and inspiration. This newfound clarity helps navigate the complexities of life, infusing each day with intention and hope. As you embrace this sense of purpose, you may discover untapped potential and the courage to pursue dreams once set aside. Purpose becomes a bridge, connecting past experiences with future possibilities.

To discover your purpose, consider engaging in reflective exercises that delve into your passions and aspirations. Begin by crafting a life purpose statement—a concise declaration that encapsulates your values, strengths, and ambitions. This statement serves as a personal manifesto, a reminder of what you wish to achieve and how you hope to impact the world. Reflect on moments when you felt most fulfilled and alive. What activities brought you joy and satisfaction? These reflections can reveal patterns and insights that guide you toward meaningful pursuits. As you refine your purpose statement, allow it to evolve with you, adapting to new experiences and insights.

Stories of others who have found renewed purpose after loss can offer inspiration and encouragement. Consider the case of a widow who channeled her grief into action by starting a nonprofit organization. Her mission was to support families facing similar losses, providing resources and community connections. Through her work, she transformed her pain into a catalyst for change, finding purpose in service to others. Her story is a testament to the power of purpose to heal and empower, illustrating how loss can become a foundation for growth and contribution. Such narratives remind us that even in the darkest moments, there lies the potential for light and transformation.

Finding meaning and purpose after loss is not a linear process. It requires patience, reflection, and a willingness to explore new facets of your identity. Engage with activities that resonate with your values and interests. Create spaces for new experiences that challenge and inspire you. As you journey through this exploration, remember that purpose is not a destination but a dynamic, evolving aspect of life. It is the thread that weaves through your actions and relationships, enriching your days with significance and fulfillment. In this pursuit, you honor both the past and the present, embracing the full spectrum of life with open arms.

Transforming Grief into Personal Growth

Grief is a profound experience that, while painful, has the potential to lead to personal growth and transformation. This concept is often referred to as post-traumatic growth, a phenomenon where individuals emerge from adversity with a renewed sense of purpose and strength. It involves moving through stages that include acknowledging the pain, finding meaning in the experience, and ultimately growing from it. These stages are never straightforward, but rather a fluid process of evolving understanding and acceptance of one's experiences. By recognizing this growth potential, you can begin to view grief not merely as a burden but as an opportunity for transformation, much like a seed that must break through the soil to grow into a strong, resilient plant.

Reframing grief as an opportunity for growth requires a shift in perspective. It involves looking at adversity not as an end but as a starting point for new possibilities. In the midst of grief, it might seem challenging to see beyond the pain, yet within every difficulty lies the potential for insight and development. Consider the moments in your life when you faced challenges and emerged stronger. These experiences often reveal untapped strengths and new pathways. By focusing on identifying growth opportunities in adversity, such as learning new skills or deepening relationships, you can transform hardship into a catalyst for positive change. This reframing process opens the door to resilience, allowing you to navigate grief with a sense of hope and purpose.

To foster growth through grief, practical strategies can provide guidance and support. One approach is to set growth-oriented goals, creating a roadmap for personal development. These goals might involve learning a new hobby, pursuing further education, or volunteering. Each step forward, no matter how small, contributes to a sense of progress and empowerment. Seeking professional guidance can also be invaluable in navigating this transformative journey. Therapists or counselors can offer tools and insights, helping you process emotions and build resilience. They provide a safe space to explore your feelings and develop strategies for growth, empowering you to take charge of your healing journey.

The long-term benefits of embracing growth through grief are profound. Enhanced resilience is one such benefit, as you develop the ability to bounce back from setbacks with greater ease and confidence. As you navigate life's challenges, this resilience becomes a wellspring of strength, allowing you to face future adversity with courage and grace. Empathy is another lasting impact, as your experiences deepen your understanding of others' struggles. This newfound empathy fosters connection and compassion, enriching your relationships and broadening your perspective. Through the lens of growth, grief becomes a teacher, imparting valuable lessons that shape your character and enrich your life.

In exploring the transformation of grief into personal growth, you embrace the possibility of emerging from darkness with renewed strength and insight. This chapter offers a framework for viewing grief as a catalyst for positive change, encouraging you to see beyond the immediate pain to the potential for growth and transformation. As you embark on this path, remember that growth is not a destination but an ongoing process of self-discovery and development. It is a journey of resilience, where each step forward is a testament to your strength and courage. As you continue to cultivate emotional and spiritual resilience, you prepare to explore the next chapter of your life, filled with new possibilities and opportunities for growth.

Conclusion

As we reach the end of this journey together, I am deeply reminded of the path we've traveled. Starting from the overwhelming challenges of widowhood, we've explored ways to confront grief, find financial independence, redefine personal identity, and build supportive networks. We've delved into strategies for practical living, embraced new opportunities, navigated new relationships, and cultivated emotional and spiritual resilience. Each chapter was crafted with the hope of guiding you through this transformative phase, offering tools and insights to help you find your footing in a new reality.

Throughout this book, we've addressed the unpredictable emotions that accompany loss and the importance of self-compassion. We've tackled the intricacies of financial management, emphasizing the empowerment that comes with understanding and organizing your finances. Together, we've explored the rediscovery of passions and interests, encouraging you to redefine who you are beyond your role as a partner. Building supportive communities has been a recurring theme, highlighting the significance of shared experiences and mutual support. We've balanced the responsibilities of daily life with the necessity of self-care and celebrated the joy of embracing new possibilities.

Navigating new relationships was approached with care, acknowledging the blend of apprehension and excitement that comes with opening your heart again. We also embraced the idea of transforming grief into personal growth, viewing it as a journey of resilience and strength rather than a mere obstacle. These experiences shape us, and I hope the insights found here continue to support you as you move forward.

Widowhood is not an endpoint. It is a chapter of transformation, filled with the potential for personal development and new beginnings. I encourage you to carry the lessons and strategies learned here into your daily life. Allow them to guide you in setting personal goals, seeking new experiences, and building connections within your community. Remember, you are not alone on this path. By sharing your own stories, you contribute to a tapestry of support and understanding, fostering a community that uplifts us all.

Reflecting on my own journey through widowhood, I am reminded of the strength and resilience that often lie dormant until we're tested. As a wife, mother, grandmother, singer, actress, missionary, and author, I have experienced the complexities of loss and the beauty of renewal. This journey has taught me that our capacity for growth and love is boundless, even in the face of adversity. It is my hope that these experiences resonate with you, offering comfort and guidance as you navigate your own path.

Now, I invite you to embrace the future with confidence and optimism. Set personal goals that excite you and seek out experiences that challenge you. Build connections within your community that inspire and support you. Continue exploring your identity and passions with courage and curiosity. Your story is unique, and by sharing it, you enrich the lives of those around you. Together, we create a tapestry of resilience and hope.

I am grateful to you for allowing me to share in your journey. It takes courage to embark on a path of healing and transformation, and I commend you for taking these steps. As you move forward, know that you possess the strength and resilience to build a fulfilling and meaningful life beyond widowhood. Embrace each day with an open heart, knowing that you are capable of overcoming any challenge that comes your way.

In the words of Helen Keller, "Although the world is full of suffering, it is also full of the overcoming of it." May this sentiment inspire you as you continue your journey, reminding you of your incredible capacity for growth and renewal. Hold on to hope, pursue joy, and know that you are never alone. Here's to new beginnings and the beautiful life that awaits you.

References

- *Coping With Grief and Loss | National Institute on Aging* https://www.nia.nih.gov/health/grief-and-mourning/coping-grief-and-loss

- *Understanding the five stages of grief* https://www.cruse.org.uk/understanding-grief/effects-of-grief/five-stages-of-grief/

- *Self-Compassion as Self-Care for Grief: How Being Kind ...* https://heatherstang.com/self-compassion-as-self-care-for-grief-meditation/

- *Grief Resource Site For Widows- The Sisterhood of Widows ...* https://sisterhoodofwidows.com/

- *Growing After Grief: Financial Independence For Widows* https://www.fa-mag.com/news/growing-after-grief--financial-independence-for-widows-78839.html

- *8 Essential Pieces of Financial Advice for Widows* https://teamhewins.com/financial-advice-for-widows/

- *7 Financial Planning Strategies for Single Women* https://smartasset.com/financial-advisor/financial-planning-for-single-women

- *Choosing the Right Financial Advisor: Considerations for ...* https://savantwealth.com/savant-views-news/article/choosing-the-right-financial-advisor-considerations-for-widows-and-widowers/

- *How to Rediscover Purpose After the Loss of a Spouse*
  https://www.psychologytoday.com/us/blog/widows-walk/202303/finding-purpose-after-the-loss-of-a-spouse

- *Living Beyond Grief: Finding New Purpose as a Widow*
  https://blog.thewellnessuniverse.com/living-beyond-grief-finding-new-purpose-as-a-widow/

- *Narrative reconstruction therapy for prolonged grief disorder ...*
  https://pmc.ncbi.nlm.nih.gov/articles/PMC4858499/#:~:text=The%20therapist%20and%20the%20patient,the%20patient's%20other%2C%20earlier%20memories.

- *Setting Goals for Grief and Loss*
  https://www.griefrefuge.com/blog/setting-goals-for-grief-and-loss

- *The Power of Widow-to-Widow Support Groups*
  https://www.grouporttherapy.com/blog/widow-to-widow-support-group

- *Regional Social Groups*
  https://soaringspirits.org/programs/in-person-programs/regional-social-groups/

- *Social Anxiety*
  https://sisterhoodofwidows.com/2022/10/31/social-anxiety/

- *10 Best Online Grief Support Groups*
  https://www.healthline.com/health/mental-health/online-grief-support-groups

- *De-Cluttering for Widows* https://sisterhoodofwidows.com/2023/10/16/de-cluttering-for-widows/

- *Reduce Stress: How to Master Time Management Skills* https://www.getharvest.com/blog/master-time-management-skills

- *Avoid Major Decision-Making While Grieving—Why This is …* https://www.jillgriefcounselor.com/blog/avoid-decision-making-while-grieving

- *5 Mental Health Rewards Of Embracing Minimalism …* https://www.forbes.com/sites/traversmark/2023/06/28/5-mental-health-rewards-of-embracing-minimalism-according-to-a-psychologist/

- *7 Ways to Release Grief from Your Body - BEST SELF* https://bestselfmedia.com/releasing-grief/

- *9 Empowering Activities I Embraced During My First Year …* https://www.nextavenue.org/9-empowering-activities-first-year-of-widowhood/

- *Solo Travel for Widows* https://navigatingwidowhood.com/2023/10/17/solo-travel-for-widows/

- *Goal Setting Steps for Widows* https://sisterhoodofwidows.com/2012/08/18/goal-steps-for-widows/

- *Coping With Grief and Loss | National Institute on Aging* https://www.nia.nih.gov/health/grief-and-mourning/coping-grief-and-loss

- *Guilt and Grief: coping with the coulda, woulda, shouldas.* https://whatsyourgrief.com/guilt-and-grief-2/

- *Dating After Being Widowed: A Guide*
  https://trustmentalhealth.com/blog/dating-after-being-widowed-a-guide

- *New relationships after the death of a partner*
  https://www.cruse.org.uk/new-relationships-after-the-death-of-a-partner/

- *How Mindfulness Builds Resilience: What Science Says*
  https://mindfulnessexercises.com/how-mindfulness-builds-resilience-what-science-says/

- *The Power of Journaling for Well-being: A Path to Self …*
  https://dhwblog.dukehealth.org/the-power-of-journaling-for-well-being-a-path-to-self-discovery-and-healing/

- *Spirituality, Inner Peace, and Well-Being*
  https://socalmentalhealth.com/spirituality-inner-peace-and-well-being/

- *18 Best Growth Mindset Activities, Worksheets, and …*
  https://positivepsychology.com/growth-mindset/

- All Biblical references are from the NIV (New International Version)